PRIME HEALING

Version 1.6

Ken Shombala Currington, M.S.

WhoKen@Gmail.com

Living Kings Productions

ISBN: 9781099932144

Imprint: Independently published

Special Thanks:
      Jen "Isha" Little- Helped to structure the writing.
      Higher Male Group- Solid Men who believe in me.
      Pete Currington- Helped with Cover.
      Izzy ivy- Illustrations.

PRIME HEALING

When your done reading some of the book, flip open your computer or your phone and dip your toes into the mystical magical world of:

www.PrimeHealing.org

It's beneficial to read the book while you are taking the online course.

PROMO-CODE: **PRIMEHEALING**

PRIME HEALING

CONTENTS

CHAPTER ONE

Diving In

Where we go One, we go All.

Okay, so if you're reading this, I'm assuming you're a human. If you're not, wow, this is a super exciting moment. I am honored to have an actual alien, reading my first book. I imagine even Earth visitors grapple with the same types of dilemmas as humans like social phobias fears and insecurities. Perhaps, like me, they don't know where their from or where their going, but are learning how to navigate the journey.

I, unlike aliens, have been in a physical body for as long as I can remember. Being a human is a deep all encompassing experience with all the things we humans are and do. We smell things, touch things, eat things ,feel things, think about things, worry about things, figure about things and do all sorts of human things. Being alive with a body has its perks and equally its challenges. But for many people, the experience of being a human has minimal "perks" and is more a game of survival. It

can feel draining and even the pleasurable stuff like relation-
ships can be a daunting and even terrible experience.

From as early as I can remember, I set out to make my
life as adventurous as possible or at least avoid conflict and my
glaring flaws. My life had had some great moments like:
teaching yoga and psychology to movie stars and rich folks in
Malibu or living in far places like Bali and India or just being
me sitting in a hammock on a sunny day wondering how this
all came to be. There's a book or two I could share about these
things, but for now, let's get back to the point of this book:

How to unblock and awaken the human energy system.

Of course there is way more than those simple words.
My objective is do dive deep into what it means to block and
awaken with stories, examples and description I hope to have
you have the experience this for yourself.

I'm going to include a bit of my story to let you know
where the ideas symbols, philosophy and tool of Prime Healing
come from.

In all my travels and studies, no matter what I did, even
during the time in which I slept in a cave for 2 months in
Northern India, I ran into the same situation:

Life feels like a game of tug-of war.

It was damned hard to keep life balanced. When I was living in Hawaii and working as a high school teacher, all seemed pretty good except that at times I didn't have enough money to buy food and put gas in my car. Even if I managed to do well for periods of my life, it seemed like I had to consistently work-harder and harder to keeping the juggling act up. And all the while having underlying nervousness, insecurities and fears pop up whenever life threw me experiences that I deemed crappy. Life wasn't bad but it wasn't all that good.

At the age of 30, I went back to school and earned an M.S in Psychology. I learned some effective tools to clear past traumas, get in tune with deep emotions and gained some expertise in the practice of counseling others from a heart-centered perspective at the University of Santa Monica. Even with all of these skills, I found myself distracted, consistently immersed in fighting off the complexities of life. What if my girlfriend left me? What if I ran out of money? Any myriad of imagined challenges would easily throw me off balance. It seemed to me that my life continually reset to being out of balance and I had to consciously work to hold it in place. Hmmm, could there be a way to allow my natural state to be in balance with myself and the world around me and to live in a state of enjoyment and trust in life? How could I flow with life instead of trying to avoid unwanted experiences and reactions?

In dedication to this pursuit, I searched with my full being to find the way into experiencing that kind of life. Around every corner, I sensed a key. Would this unlock the door?

Maybe if I put all of these together, they'll link up and I'll finally be at the right frequency, or somehow magically get the password and that will let me be at peace.

During my quest, I explored systems like Kundalini Yoga, in which I would wake up at three in the morning to chant, practice intensive breathing exercises and a variety of transformative yoga postures. The phrase, "Happy - Healthy - Holy" is often used to describe the state of being one reaches and maintains with regular practice and it seemed attainable and sustainable when I offered my entire being with full effort and absolute commitment to the path. So, I dove in and after six months, I dove out.

I don't remember the exact moment when I decided to renounce the practice, I remember thinking, "This just isn't my path." I'm a fourth-generation New Yorker and I didn't want to have to wear all white, change my name and be within the confines of a strict monastic lifestyle to maintain happiness. I felt secure in my decision to put in the hard work but the entire paradigm of constant practice and fierce diligence didn't quite make sense to me. My quest was to reach a state of grace and ease, enjoying the fullness of my life experience and not constantly work at keeping myself in tune. Upon grounding this realization, I refocused my energy and aligned myself to my personal truth, allowing that to guide me. As the path unfolded, I attended transformational seminars, intensive breathing workshops and a myriad of classes. I read countless books, learned and engaged in a variety of yogic practices and ex-

plored the realms of alternate states more times than I can remember.

I enjoyed doing these things, but I still had this feeling of a pebble in my shoe. Things popped up from every direction, demanding my attention, draining my energy, pulling me off balance. I'd lose sense of direction and focus, with my mind centered on survival and mundane challenges in one moment and then fully engaged in some relationship drama or career obstacle the next. Life didn't feel like a mythical adventure. It felt like a grind.

The next big stop on my crusade was The HeartMath Institute. If you've never heard of it and even if you are an alien, you should really check this group of talented and heart-centered people out: www.HeartMath.com . Simply put, Heart-Math is the science of positive emotions and their impact on the human system via the heart-brain connection. The research team at HeartMath has found that there are more seats to consciousness than just the brain, discovering that the mind functions as a unified system throughout the entire body, with a surprisingly elegant part of it operating in the heart. They use their proprietary biofeedback software to develop ways in which we can utilize deep breathing to generate positive emotions that create a heart rhythm that resonates a healing effect on every cell of the body. They even have a device that can be linked to a computer or phone that shows, in real-time the beat to beat changes of the heart rhythm or heart rhythm vari-

ability. This practice of biofeedback induces states heartbeat coherence and effects the entire body.

"Bam! There it is." I was convinced I had found the philosopher's stone. All I had to do was to keep my breath in coherence with positive emotions and my heart rhythm would naturally be synced with the flow of life. I remember how much I enjoyed working with the HeartMath program. The 5-10 minute sessions on the biofeedback program quickly helped me dial myself into balance. Every time I completed a session, I recognized the effects. It felt so good to be in sync with myself and to this day, these sessions are one of my favorite exercises for de-stressing and re-centering myself. HeartMath has an excellent program. Recognizing its value, I chose to attend a week-long training program in the mountains of Santa Cruz and became a HeartMath certified trainer. They have implemented their revolutionary training programs in schools with incredible results and it's my opinion that most schools would benefit greatly from emotional intelligence training at all grade levels. Here is a link to their programs and studies: https://www.heartmath.org/education/classroom-programs/

I continued training with HeartMath and gained significant benefits along the way, but even so, there was still something missing. I still was in a game of tug-of-war with all the aspects of my multifaceted life. Sometimes I was winning, sometimes I was losing and regardless of the outcome, I kept my grip tight at my end the rope, unwilling to let go, fearing

that if I did, I would end up poor, sick, alone, homeless or just lost in the world.

I kept feeling that life was too complex to figure out and demanded my unwavering effort to keep balanced. "Like a foolish man who built his house on the sand....". Life was shifting sand beneath me in an ocean of change while I was constantly calculating how to avoid pain. The rest of this passage reads, "Everyone therefore who hears these words of mine and does them, I will liken him to a wise man, who has built his house on a rock. The rain came down, the floods came and the winds blew and beat on that house; and it didn't fall, for it was founded on the rock." (Matthew 7:24-27) I was looking for my rock. I had no idea what it was or what it looked like, but I wanted that stability.

After finishing my degree in psychology, I worked at a yoga and wellness retreat center in Malibu, California called The Ashram. It was, and is, a great retreat center dedicated to immersing its participants in a week-long program of yoga, hiking, massage, workouts and pool volleyball, all fueled by organic vegetarian food and inspiring activities from sunup till sundown. During my time as a trainer I interacted with many wealthy and successful people. During the daily 10-12 mile hikes, I spoke with the guests about their lives and their views on the world. One thing they did have in common was some degree of financial stability. Was money the rock I was looking for...was that the answer? It seemed logical that if I could figure out the money game, I would finally have the stability and cen-

tered relaxed presence I had been searching for. Or, was Noto-rious BIG right? "Mo' Money, Mo' Problems...?" It seemed worth finding out.

Liberation Training

At the age of thirty-two, I left my sweet home at The Ashram in Malibu and set off for Hawaii. I had been inspired with the idea of developing a yogic system for unlocking the magic of money. After wandering around the island for several months, I found myself moving into a beautiful home with my then-girlfriend and took a job as the lead teacher at Baldwin High School's CBI special education program. I would spend the next few years mentoring and teaching beautiful young humans with learning challenges while writing and compiling the details of what would later become a work I've developed called "Liberation Training."

www.LiberationTraining.com

Liberation Training and The Liberation Equation was my opus. Of course, you can go take the course to gain a fuller understanding of Liberation Training, but in short, the main idea is that one can transform conflict into power. To do this, we can see that anything that upsets us is in direct and polar conflict with our core values. For example, if you are a nature lover or even just someone who is concerned to the current state of the planet and you are walking in the woods when you come across a bulldozer tearing up the ground, ripping apart

groves of trees, annihilating life and devastating the ecosystem, you will most likely feel intense emotions arise. From where exactly does this reaction originate? Why do we get triggered? In this framework, we see that it occurs because what you are witnessing is in deep conflict with your core values. The core value that places caring for, respecting, valuing and preserving the "Balance and Power of Nature" as a core belief or high priority.

Instead of staying in conflict, you could choose to utilize the Liberation Equation to release the emotion, energy and power you feed into the conflict. Instead, you can claim that same energy to empower your own personal set of core values. The reclaimed energy is guided to empower the value you hold that is in conflict with scenes of deforestation. The preservation of the "Pristine Balance and Power of Nature" is the resonant core belief eliciting the strong reaction. Moving from reaction to response gives the opportunity for an informed, embodied and wisely chosen action. In an empowered place, you're able to choose right action instead of knee-jerk reaction. This simple yet powerful energy technique allows the practitioner to transform conflicted energy into empowerment and take centered and clear steps towards right action. Below is the steps of Liberation training. Again, for a clear description of the steps go to LiberationTraining.com.

Liberation Equation

Step 1- Conflicts

Be aware when you feel something that creates mental or emotional tension within you.

Step 2- Source

Use your Intention to connect to Source **"I am…......**
….."

Step 3- Feel Conflict Deeper

After you center yourself, feel back into the tension. Be truthful and open to feel as much as you can.

Step 4- Source

Return to Source using   **"I am…........**

Then say- "And the truth is..I put my power into this situation."

Step 5- Free the Energy " Popping Bubbles"

-Imagine the situation like Bubbles-

" Because I put my Power into this situation

I now Free It! "

- As you Free the Conflict- Flick your fingers on both hands and breathing out.
- Imagine all the elements of the situation like Bubbles and Pop them.

Step 6- Breathe the Energy Back Into Core-Values

Once the bubbles burst take a deep breath.
Feel the Energy returning back into you. Feel it back
in your body.

Step 7- Appreciation who you truly are- Core-Values

" I am so **thankful** for this whole situation because it has allowed me to be more of who I truly am"

(I am) ....is ..(Core-Value)......... "

*Take a moment to feel your current state. Breathing in
and out of the heart and feel what it is like to release
the tension of conflict and have your Core-Values empowered. Maintain a Grateful feeling and get ready
to feel Wow as life unfolds!*

The success of this work required working the practice,
just like so many other tools and techniques. After about two
years into developing Liberation Training, I recall getting all of
the steps into a coherent format, feeling the imminent completion of the program on the horizon. I was four months into
working as a teacher in the CBI (Community-Based Instruc-
tion) program at the local public high school, operating beyond
maximum capacity on a daily basis. I recall feeling maxed out
mentally, physically and emotionally, overwhelmed with all the
meetings and paperwork, doing my best to juggle two class-

rooms of over thirty students all demanding my attention and focus. I was working 6 days a week and on top of getting very close to reaching burnout, my girlfriend left me. I had barely enough money to cover our $1200 monthly rent and meet my basic needs. I was overwhelmed and felt entirely worn out, stretched beyond my capacity.

I remember walking the trail along the taro fields where my home was. This was an idyllic expanse of land in West Maui where me and my landlord's home was. The 5000-acre macadamia nut farm had a river an old-growth forest and immeasurable numbers of beings and animals living off of the abundant offerings the lush jungle provided. With the $1200 to cover the full rent in my hand on my way to pay my landlord, I noticed the closer I got, the more everything began boiling up inside me.

I stopped. It was all too much. The pressure had pulled me too far off-center. I was working way too hard to just barely pay my rent. I didn't have the time or means to support a move to a smaller place and I really liked my home. I was alone- I was stressed- I was broke. My mind was swirling in conflict so I just stopped walking. I had been writing and training in conflict resolution but it was tough to remember it all when the stress and emotions took over. I stood there, completely immobilized. I was done. I was so done and then I thought, "Well, what if I'm actually just done with all this, I might as well give this Liberation Training thing a shot. Okay, fine I'll use the Liberation Equation.

Step 1-

Feel it fully.

"Oh, yeah... I feel the conflict. This sucks! I work so freaking hard and I have nothing! No Money. No Time. No Energy. No Nothing! AUGH!..."

Witness the feelings.

"Yup, there it is, I definitely feel the conflict."

Step 2-

Connect to Source with my personal Intention.

"Okay, okay... I'll say it..... : 'I AM INFINITY."

I was surprised to admit it but that actually did really shift something.

Step 3-

Deepen into the feeling of conflict.

"Yup, I can feel deeper into this...The School...The Money...The Rent. The Girlfriend Leaving. Eating terrible food in the cafeteria.... So unfair! This is terrible!!! Why does life have to be so hard?!"

Step 4-

Okay back to Source...Using my intention statement.

"I AM INFINITY".

I could feel the truth at work. I could feel the gripping anger in my belly releasing. My breathe was deeper and could feel a tingling in my hands.

Step 5-

<u>Freeing the energy, popping bubbles (visualization of the issue around me):</u>

"I put my Power into all of this. Now, I release the school, money, rent, everything! Whew !!!!!"

Step 6-

<u>Breathing the released energy back in:</u>

"Ahh, yes, I feel the energy I put into this situation coming back to me. I am breathing it back into my body, deep into my chest, into my core. Yes! I am Grounded. I am Energized. I am on my Path."

Step 7-

<u>Completing the exercise with gratitude, affirming the self and core values:</u>

" I am deeply grateful for this whole situation with the school, my house, even the rent, because it has allowed me to get my power back and become more of who I truly am."

–

Wow! In that moment, things really shifted. I was standing in exactly the same spot with all the same situations with $1200 in an envelope and I felt completely different. I was grateful for everything. I was on the right path. I felt the liberation. I continued on to my landlord's house and met up with him in the back of his home. I handed him the rent and told him I was so happy to be here and that I felt grateful for my home. He stood there holding the envelope of cash and asked, " Are you still teaching at the high school? "Yup, it's tough work but I love it," I replied. He continued with clear concern, "And now you're paying the full rent on your own". "Yes, well, us ending our relationship was a hard transition but it's for the best," I shared. "Well, let's lower your rent," he continued. "I can't imagine it's easy for a teacher like you to pay all these bills all on your own. Let's just take your rent down to $750."

My whole being lit up. I took a deep breath and said, "Thanks, I deeply appreciate that." As I left, I felt a rush. Not from the money but from a "holy crap!" moment at the realization that Liberation Training was real! It really worked! I stopped and ran the equation again to clear the situation deeper. I felt the shift. When I got home, two friends called me and asked me to come out for dinner in Wailuku. I thought to myself, "Sure... I have $450 bucks. I can afford to go out and celebrate!"

We went to a local pizza place and were having a great time. Our server was super cute. One of my friends encouraged me to ask her out. I thought, "Why not?...I'm single and she

seems like fun." I asked her out and the next day she came over to the property after work. We walked up by the river and talked about life. She told me that she really wanted to move to this side of the island but it was really hard to find a place. I told her that I had the whole house to myself and it was pretty much empty almost every day. Since it's warm every night I was sleeping in the big carport in the garden and the bedroom was open. Her eyes lit up and we ran back to the house. She was blown away. " I can really live here!" she shouted. I said she could pay whatever she felt was fair. She said $700 would be an incredible deal. She moved in the next day. I had a great new friend and my rent was now 50 bucks!

I can honestly say that from that point in 2008 forward, I have rarely if ever, worried about money. I have had lots of money and almost none, but I am steady with running the equation. Was this it? Was this my rock? Was this the place from which I could release the tug-of-war rope and just be me? I think you can feel for yourself as you read this what the answer is to that question. It's a damn good technique and inspired parts of Prime Healing. I still use it and teach Liberation Training but no, it's not my rock. I have another great tool in my bag and it's something I am very proud to share. But I knew my rock was out there and I was off to find it.

www.LiberationTraining.com Check out the online course.

With the Liberation Training program complete, I left my safe home in Maui and set out to see what was next in the world. With my ability to transform conflicted energy around

money into creative power, I started many business ventures over the next few years. I worked with my brother in Thailand and started an online herbal company that is still successfully going to this day KeterWellness.com. I also started the company, TruthPaste.com and did over three years of research and development into how to use herbal extracts infused in oil to deeply clean teeth. That company is still doing well and is getting ready to go into full production. Other business ventures failed and cost me a lot of money and time, but was able to rebound quickly with the Liberation Training tools. In early 2017, I helped to merge two machine companies and helped form an engineering and machine company called TruSteel.com. It was funny how my two main companies both had the concept of truth in their names without me naming either one of them. Truth was indeed what I was seeking, but I was still finding that life was inherently hard to keep balanced. During this time, I was using what I learned from my training in psychology, coaching and counseling to assist clients with their issues. I was agile at helping others but looking back, at that point in time, there was never enough I could offer others or even to myself to allow the natural ease of being a human to be the baseline experience.

Near the end of 2018, I was introduced to a very unusual healer. She was very sensitive and adept at reading human energy fields. I had worked with many healers before including indigenous shamans of Peru, hands-on healers and a multitude of energy workers. She was different, very direct and clear

in her ability to read imbalances in human energy fields. I would go to her office/temple almost every day to sit with her. On most days, she would say that I had a lot of potential but that my energy field was muddled because I was unconsciously attached to others. Over the next few months, I committed to remaining consciously aware of my thoughts and diligently cleared my energetic field any time I witnessed an attachment or leak. I practiced HeartMath, Liberation Training and long periods of deep meditation. I spent time tuning in to myself and took solitary walks in nature and yet when I would sit with her, she could point out where my system was still leaking or tied into others. I was determined to figure out how to be a clear human, so I continued to work harder and harder to reach a state of freedom.

In early February of 2019, a group of healers and myself set off to Las Vegas to assist this energy reader in giving a class at the Luxor Casino. I know to some it might seem like an unusual place to do healing work, but in the darkness of the chaos and debauchery of Las Vegas, the light is even brighter. We rented one of the top floors of the Luxor Pyramid and I assisted in a beautiful sound and energy healing ceremony. It was a great event but I was beginning to feel restless. Maybe the only way to keep on the path was perpetual work. That in itself felt intense and daunting as my inspiration for continuing the process of awakening in this way was diminishing.

Our plan was to leave Las Vegas after the event and move on to the Tucson Gem show. Frustration was bubbling up

from deep inside me and I realized I really just wanted to be finished with all this work. I couldn't see the point of all this clearing work if the complexities of life, money and relation-ships just threw me off center again and again. I talked with my teacher about this. After I shared my feelings of frustration, she changed our trajectory. She tuned in with the moment and told me that instead of going as planned to the gem show, we were going to rent a room at Caesar's Palace and experience the high energy of Chinese New Year.

We checked into Caesar's Palace amongst the crowds of people getting ready for the big celebration that evening. The casino at the Palace was electric and opulent, decorated with mythical Chinese dragons, the walls and ceiling dripping with ornamental flags in the traditional colors of gold and red, all chosen to amplify the energy of luck and prosperity. We got to the room around sunset and I was blown away watching the deep red and orange sunset of the Nevada desert from the forty-second floor right above the Bellagio fountain. My teacher is a very private person and rarely goes out in public but not on this night. We got dressed up and first went out for an all-you-can-eat seafood buffet. We laughed and talked as we ate plates of crab, sushi and everything from the ocean that we could ever want.

After finishing our royal meal, we headed to the lobby to meet one of my teacher's top student. We walked through the vibrant casino amongst many Asian guests dressed in tuxedos and formal dresses to find a man named Yan in the big open

marble entrance ways. Yan is Polynesian and built like a truck with dark skin and big tattoos on his arms, but all that pales in comparison to his huge laugh and crushing hugs. We all headed back to the casino and Yan began to describe to me how the high energy builds in certain parts of the casino, especially on Chinese New Year. He told me that when the energy is really high like this and you become still, you can experience a heightened state of connection.

We passed by packed poker tables and the endless rows of high stakes slot machines. People were out to have the time of their lives. The energy of "wow" was palpable. The night was really picking up momentum as the time approached midnight. When we got to the center of the casino, both my teacher and Yan stopped and said, "This is the spot." We all tuned in to the field. It was electric. Yan walked up to me, told me to close my eyes and he put his hand on my head. He told me to relax and breathe deep and slow. In a flash, so many things passed through me. It felt like every lesson, every meditation, every teaching and every moment in a flash finally made sense. I felt clear and at ease. I felt all at once that the simple answer to my search had been given and realized. I had the simple visual of a dark cube below me and a radiating light above me. In that moment those two symbols had deep meaning and were embedded with vast knowledge. I experienced that when all is accepted at the Base the Crown opens its connections. I knew my quest for my rock had met its pinnacle moment. The game of tug-of-war, the struggle for balance and my deep desire to feel

okay was complete. My rock was there firmly below me! The stability I felt was real. I had endured the long journey and for the first time felt I complete. I looked at my teacher and when our eyes met, she said, "Ahhh, now you are clear."

After some time, I realized this was now my new normal. As I tuned in, I discovered that I was enjoying feeling freer than I'd ever felt and at the same time, I was feeling even more connected. Instead of those two things being distinct opposites, I now had the capacity for both sides of reality at once. I was perfect and I was a mess. I was fake and was living my unfolding truth. I was constantly changing but could also feel below me a place that never changed and was here before this world and will be hereafter.

The end of the tug-of-war when one can simply trust that whatever life brings they can be with and experience in its wholeness. The world opens up to us as we discover our deep unchanging power and we get to enjoy life in a much more ease-full, fulfilling and joyful way.

I want to share this simple process that clears the complexities of life and allows the real reason we are on Earth to unfold. I call this process "Prime Healing" because to me it is the core mechanism that allows everything else in life to work. Prime Healing doesn't interfere with other healing techniques. Instead, it is a simple initial process that makes all techniques more potent, effective and enduring in their effect. It is a process of allowing all of life to be experienced.

CHAPTER TWO

Basics of Prime Healing

*"Out beyond ideas of wrong and right,
there is a field. I'll meet you there."* -**Rumi**

Is there a place in you that is sovereign? Is there a place in you right now, that is free from right and wrong, good and bad? Is there a space in you that is free from money, relationships and all the doings of this world?

Prime Healing lays out the steps for each of us to have the shift in awareness that unveils our sovereign self to ourselves. Prime Healing is a shift that allows a deep and steady activation that is unique for each of us. Through story, examples, meditation and description of the process, I'll guide you into the experience of this shift for yourself. You may also access the video series on Prime Healing available at PrimeHealing.org, along with additional resources.

It's helpful to have an overview of this work before we dive into the details of how we practice it. It never ceases to amaze me how intrinsically simple this work is. Yet, for the work to amplify our capacity to function and thrive, we must

make fundamental changes in the way we operate. Experiencing it for yourself is the only way you can grasp this work, there are no shortcuts. This journey calls us forward to step into the next iteration of ourselves, sovereign, inspired, awake, self-possessed and self-directed.

Prime Healing is the process of unveiling our sovereignty by releasing blocks from the base of our energetic system and reconnecting from the top of our energetic system.

Yup, that's it. Close the book because all your worries and problems are over...

You are still reading and assume that it's not that simple. Indeed, to master this way of being, we must dive deep into the ocean of ourselves and be willing to be completely vulnerable to feeling all of our fear, shame, guilt and nightmares.

With Prime Healing, you will have a clear map that will instruct you on how to do the work to become free and connected. Before we go further, let's define some key terms we will use often in this book while going through the process of Prime Healing.

Key Terms of Prime Healing

Sovereign: Webster's dictionary: One that exercises supreme authority within a limited sphere.

In Prime Healing this is symbolized by the cube and is located at our base just below our seat. When we are open to fully experiencing everything the Base is unblocked and flowing in and up.

It is the place in you that is only for you, not affected by anything in this world. No person, nor situation has influence here. Allowing us to experience everything and to still have a place that is untouched and unchanging.

Base: Located approximately two feet below the seat, The Base is the energetic root of sovereignty.

Symbols: The language of images that connect the conscious mind to the sub-conscious mind.

Cube: The symbol to connect our conscious minds to the place in us that is sovereign and only for us.

Base Attachments or Blocks: These are the blocks which we have placed on ourselves because we are not able to be with challenging emotions or experiences. Base Attachments are usually present in an effort to protect us from pain, inadvertently leaving one easily affected and destabilized by situations. What we resist persists. Theses blocks are called "attachments" because it is our own attachments to avoiding fully feeling these blocks that keep them in place.

Attachments are released by accepting the pain that have been blocked and absorbed back into the energetic system via the base cube.

Duality- When two (dual), realities (ity) are happening at the same time. "I am fake and bringing truth."

Base Energetics: How our system is either sovereign and clear at the base or blocked and corded to external situations. Prime Healing shows how to be with blocks, release them and allow the energy to flow in and up our energetic system.

Crown: The symbol for this center is a small sun. This radiant light, which is set about two feet above the head connects to everything.

Sun: Symbol to connect with our Crown

Prime Healing: This is the process of releasing blocks from the Base and sitting on our throne of sovereignty. In this state we can accept all parts of our world, even the difficult and frightening things. We connect to life through the Crown, granting us a deep trust in ourselves and in life.

King or Queen: When you are sitting on your sovereign throne with your Crown open. The place where good and bad are in

their natural harmony. When all is unblocked and flowing through our system.

Whole Truth- The state of realizing that all experiences are in duality. The Whole Truth is revealed when energies like anxiety and relaxation are seen as equals, fluctuating through our experience.

The Whole Truth unveils itself when we unblock the wholeness in any situation.

Imagine having the ability to experience a balanced state where everything in and out of you was in harmony. Empowering you to be clear, connected and sovereign.

What if everything you have experienced in your entire life and have up until this point deemed good, bad, mixed or otherwise, were key components in the book of answers you've been seeking on your quest for peace, joy and freedom? What if life has been granting your wishes all along? What if healing wasn't a laborious process but rather simply just the gathering of stuck experiences and releasing them with one breath? I think it is time me, you, and all of humanity had such a tool.

It is the intention of this process to help you gather every memory, emotion and experience that is stuck in you, realize that this stagnation is simply places that you are unable to be fully with, free the blocks and allow them to flow back in door of the Base and connect via the Crown.

Have you ever had the experience of being in a relationship and at some point you both begin pulling on one another energetically? It can become a struggle to find a balance in the relationship and the smallest things can cause a blow-up. It becomes obvious from the teachings of Prime Healing that the couple's Base Energetics are deeply attached. So often, in long-term relationships unconscious attachments begins to tug on one another. There arises from within the subtleties of the relationship an unspoken agreement that says, "If you give me energy from down there, I'll give you energy from down there. Then we are safe and connected." As life continues, one of these people might say, "Okay, I need more," and in turn they might be met with the same feelings from their partner. Now, who gets the energy? Each wants the energy, feels deserving of it and is doing their best to get it. When the great game of Tug-of-War begins, the attachments pull and push, energies entangle further and the struggle continues.

For example, lets say one partner felt neglected by there parents when they were a child. If they have not yet fully embraced the experience of neglect they have blocks in their energetic system. If they feel that their partner is neglecting them they might go into a defensive reaction at the first signs of neglect. Tugging at their partner and insisting that it is their fault for causing them to feel this way. Instead of being sovereign at the Base and being open to experiencing neglect they set limits and demand that their partner treat them differently.

After seeing this pattern so many times, I began to witness that humans are residing in a loop. With all my new clients, it has been necessary to first teach them why it is beneficial to release all Base Attachments or blocks. It took some time before new clients realized for themselves that Base Energetics don't effectively manage the complexities of life. It has been rewarding to see them shift into a better way of connecting with parents, friends, money, relationships with a sovereign Base. It was inspiring to see freedom and joy emanating from their beings and it was clear to me that this was working. So I decided to stop repeating myself with each individual and write a book instead. I am writing this book so that people can learn for themselves how this process works. I am more of a speaker than a writer, but I am fully committed to making this information available in an easy read book.

Let's explore a metaphoric story that provides some insight into how Prime Healing works. Imagine an alternate reality in which everyone drives their cars backward. All the streets have been designed for driving this way. Your driving examiner ensured that you knew how to throw your arm over the passenger seat to twist around backward. You passed the driving test and were just as good as anyone else at looking behind the car as you drove around town. All was peachy keen in backward driving land. Speed limits max out at 10 on the highways and accidents happen at every corner. This is a metaphor for the results of using the Base to navigate our lives. Then comes the day when one brave person discovers forward driving. Oh, this

is so different. This might even feel scary at first but it's so much easier. Wow! Turning is so easy and there's no need for twisting around. This feels so much more comfortable! The struggle of driving turns into a thrill and suddenly it's an experience of speed and agility. This isn't actually hard at all. Yes, this is a metaphor for connecting to life through the Crown. Although you may have become accustomed to the struggles of tug-of-war, it is now time to feel the thrill of life as you learn to drive your machine.

Base Energetics aren't fit to navigate our decisions and life. They get muddled and mixed and when operating from this place, humans are automatically reactionary, on the defense and on the offense. When we feel tugged at our Base, we feel unstable, like any move could topple us over. Feeling unsafe and unstable, we can then easily revert to attempting to control the world around us to create a false sense of security. Put a group of people in this state together and you'll see chaos, like all the wars being waged around the world.

We are beings of choice and as such, we are ultimately choosing to continue this pattern well past the phase that worked for us in childhood. We co-created this pattern with our caregivers to ensure our needs were met in infancy and we continued to utilize this method as life unfolded, tugging our way along, grasping and giving and ultimately having a rather rough go of it. Like a child crying for there Mom's attention, we continue to cry for attention as adults.

Now, it is your time to choose. If you knew how to shift into freedom and make your Base sovereign, would you make the shift? Do you want to keep playing tug-of-war with your life? Or, are you ready to let go of the rope and return to that simple powerful state in which your connection to self is solid and everything is exactly as it should be?

CHAPTER THREE

Base & Crown

"I have no answers just my perspective on how me and you can look into the mystery of life and say wow!"

-Prime Healing

Let's pause for a moment before we get more into the steps of Prime Healing. It makes sense here to give you a deeper experience of this work. Theories about cubes, spheres, the Base and Crown don't really make any real impact unless you can sense or feel on a deeper level what is happening to you while doing this work. So let's drop right into the first guided meditation.

Introduction to Prime Breathing

This exercise will offer you an introduction to the process of Prime healing. The practice encompasses within it all of the codes for Prime Healing even if you don't yet fully understand the inner workings of the process yet. This is an easy breathing practice that will allow you to start sensing the trans-

formative power of this work. It is not necessary for your mind to be cognizant of the mechanics and in some ways, it could be very beneficial for a beginning practitioner to have the first encounter with the work to be from a place of feeling rather than from an intellectual perspective.

Prime Breathing is described in great detail in later chapters but for now, I will just walk you through an introduction to it.

Guided Meditation (For Video www.PrimeHealing.org)

-Sit in a comfortable position.

-Start by becoming aware of your breath.

-As you follow your breath, allow it to deepen. Feel each inhalation and exhalation and allow the time between each of your breaths to extend a bit longer.

-On the next deep exhale, relax your body.

-On the inhale bring your awareness just below your butt to your Base. Imagine you are sitting on a big dark cube. Like a stone cube that is your personal throne. Like a king or queen sitting on your stone throne.

-Deeply inhale and imagine the cube like a vacuum, drawing all of the energy into your Base, this stable space below your seat. Feel the density and stability becoming more palpable with each inhale. Continue long deep breathing into your Base. You can close your eyes for a moment. When you can sense and visualize the Cube at the Base then continue to the next step.

-On the next inhale into the Base, pause and bring your awareness all the way up the center of your body to about 1-2 feet above your head. Breathe out from your Crown and feel the energy radiating and connecting out in every direction. Imagine breathing out from the center of a small sun above your head.

-Breathing in, feel yourself vacuuming everything into the solid black cube throne below you. Pause for a moment while you quickly move your awareness up through the central channel to the area above your head. As you breathe out see light radiating out in every direction, like a small sun shining in every direction.

-Inhale into the Base. Pause and bring awareness up the body and two feet above your head. Breathe out from the small sun above your head.

-Repeat at your own pace for two or more cycles with your eyes closed. (really close your eyes and do 2 cycles)

-Then stop, allow yourself to feel what you feel. This state is what makes Prime Healing work. Make the Base sovereign and open the crown. The process is simple yet deep.

-Feel how present you are with only a few minutes of attention. You are both sovereign and connected, your power easily amplified at any time by your intention and breath.

For the rest of the day and tomorrow, practice Prime Breathing at least twice a day. Here is the quick and easy out-line of the process:

-Breath in through the Base. Imagine the dark stone cube throne.

-Bring your awareness up toward the crown.

-Breathe out through the Crown. From a small white radiating sun

-Breathe in the Base.

-Bring awareness up.

-Breathe out through the Crown.

-Use your hands to follow the pattern.

-After three cycles relax and feel the Base and the Crown

This work is not merely a mental imagination exercise, but rather a process to be experienced by your mental, physical and emotional bodies. This experience can be done easily through the breath, utilizing feeling, emotional sensitivity and energetic awareness.

Prime Breathing will function as the activator of your energetic realignment in the upcoming Prime Healing process. Throughout the process, when we clear Base Attachments, activate connection to life from the Crown and go through the four ceremonies, we will have the opportunity to practice this new ability. Being able to clear and activate your energy field with this simple breathing practice will help you activate and work the process. It will support you on your way to knowing the full truth of yourself. This tool, your breath, is readily available whenever you call upon it.

The videos at PrimeHealing.org will help you get the hang of Prime Breathing.

The Base

"I declare that my Base is only for me; sovereign and complete."

On that day in February in Vegas with Yan's hands on my head, as every speck of dust cleared from my life all I could see was a cube below me and a bright light above. As I worked with these new tools, it became clear that the cube was the symbol of sovereignty. It is just a symbol pointing at something in you that you might feel to be true, " That we are free and powerful and here for a purpose." I want to share this symbol with you.

To do this visualize a black cube, heavy and still, settled about two to three feet below your seat. Prime Healing utilizes the shape of the cube because the symbol represents stability and allows us to access the place in us that is sovereign. The

visualization exercise will help your mind and body sense the area below you and activate the experience of sovereignty.

At first, it might seem strange. Hmm, what is this black cube thing? I was a little shy about sharing it at first too. But after a while, it started to make sense. A dark dense throne that in the subconscious world could slow light down and allow my base to take in everything in the world. Like my own little black hole that could if I chose to take in everything and slow all the patterns down and begin a transformative process.

I was able to access this moment of deep clarity over and over again by using the symbol of the cube. Symbolic language has been used by shamans in many cultures to access the subconscious world. Our frontal cortex keeps us connected to our normal functioning state. We use language to communicate in our conscious world. The subconscious world is connected to everything and uses symbols to communicate. To connect our conscious world to our subconscious world, shamans and now us neo-shamans, use symbols.

The Peruvian tradition of the Q'ero-Mesa use animal symbols to tap into the subconscious world and use the power of the interconnected nature of reality to perceive deeper aspects of reality. To do this they simply imagine or look at an image of the animal. With this image in the frontal cortex, they then send this image to the base of their brain, this happens automatically. The image is now acting as a bridge from the conscious brain to the subconscious world. Then they wait for symbols or information to come back to the conscious mind.

"We live in a world of symbols and images where spirit and commonplace are one… Understanding comes from the heart, and is perceived in the moment." -Lame Deer, Sioux Shaman

Let's go through an example of how symbolic language works from the Q'ero-Mesa tradition. This exploration of symbolic language will let you see why using the Cube and the Sun are so potent in Prime Healing.

Let's say you are buying a car. A row of cars are in front of you and you want to know first the facts and figures with no emotion. For this, you would use, in the Q'ero-Mesa tradition, the snake. You visualize the snake and allow the gates of perception to open. Symbols of the engine and smoke come back. Not a good sign. Pass on this car. Next car. Visualize the snake in the mind and wait. You may see the snake and it looks vibrant. Good sign. Let's explore this car further. Next is the Jaguar. Primal power and sexuality. You look at the car and bring the image of the jaguar to the mind. Impulses of power and yes come back. Jaguar is happy. Next the hummingbird. Hummingbird is the symbol to connect with happiness and longevity. You might imagine the hummingbird and images of rainbows come back. Ahh good signs. By using the bridges to the interconnected world with the animals you are able to quickly narrow your search down and perhaps get the best car that is perfectly suited for you. Just for your curiosity here is a list of the animals used in the Q'uero-Mesa tradition.

Snake - Facts and figures without emotion. Always use snake first to gather all the facts about a person, situation or thing. Located at the base of the spine.

Jaguar- Primal Power and sexuality. If the jaguar sends good signals then there is vibrant energy there. Located just below the belly-button.

Hummingbird- Happiness and Longevity. Will I be happy with this situation for a long time? When the hummingbird sends back positive symbols then there is a good chance happiness will be there. Located at the solar plexus.

Eagle or Condor- Seeing the bigger picture. Soaring above the situation. The Eagle/Condor Allows us to see the bigger picture and how this choice or situation connects to the bigger picture. Located at the center of the chest.

Black Triangle also known as Huascar - The black triangle lets us see everything we don't know. Possibility of accidents, unseen problems or something unknown that could be of great benefit. Using the image of the Black triangle we open up to this information. Located at the center of the throat.

Dragon or the Quetzacoatal- The winged serpent opens up the power of all the previous channels at the same time. It is like a snake, hummingbird, jaguar, condor and black triangle combined. It is the final analysis. If the Dragon is vibrant and the symbols come back from the subconscious world positive you have a clear path ahead. Located in the center of the head above the eyes.

<u>Sun or Pacha Cuti</u>- This symbol is a bright ball of light shining in all directions. It connects us to the light in every-thing. It is located just above the head.

To use these tools it is a process of training the mind to use the images and then wait for a response. A busy or distract-ed mind will muddle communication. A trusting and still mind will deepen these connections and get clear communication from the conscious mind to the subconscious mind.

In Prime Healing we use the symbol of the Cube. By imagining the cube it allows us to access the place in the sub-conscious world that slows down light. When light of any form is drawn into the cube it slows down and becomes fundamen-tal material or clear light. When the density of the cube reduces all form to clear light, it then travels to its opposite, the Crown. The Cube's ability to vacuum in and melt everything allows it to be a place unaffected by anything in this world.

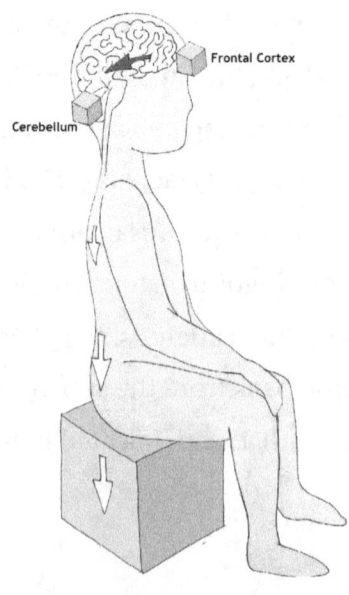

If you recall from the first chapter, I had been on a quest to find "my rock". Well, this is the rock. This is the stone, the key to my quest. It was what I had been looking for all along and it was in me, sovereign and complete, the Base upon which everything else could be built. When I slow down my busy world and see the cube below me I allow my sovereign throne to envelope me. When I let go of the rope, I stop participating in the game of good and bad and nothing is capable of pulling on me. From my throne I can see that all the world is in polarity. Good and evil reside in one another. That my greatest fears are unveiling my highest dreams. A sense of deep gratitude for everything fills me as I sit on my sovereign throne humble and exalted, with an open heart, waiting for the sun to rise in us all.

The Crown

Now that you have an initial understanding about the concept of the Base, let's explore the Crown. The Crown is the area just above your head. If the Base is one point, the Crown, as it's mirror opposite, is all points. If the Base is closed and complete, the Crown is open and connected. Light, dark, you get the picture, opposites.

The symbol you can visualize is a three-dimensional small sun at the Crown, a sphere of bright white light. The light of the Crown is imbued with the wisdom of all of the energetic centers (chakras) of the body and it is the best way to connect to the world with all of its complexities and awesomeness.

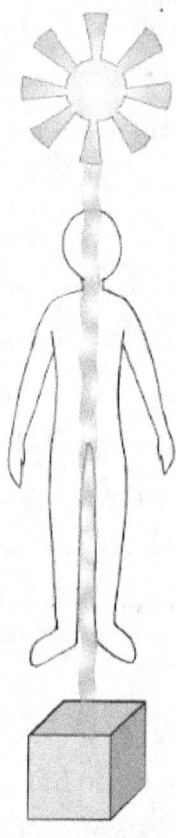

Using the symbol of the sun we enter into the place in us that flows out in all directions and connects to everything.

While the Base is solid and heavy, the Crown is light, bright, open and able to utilize the wisdom gathered from the energetic centers traversing the central channel. When the Crown is open, we enjoy a more interconnected experience and a more truthful experience. This is what some Native Americans describe as the silver threads that interconnect us all. The Hopis speak of a Spider Grandmother who, conscien-

tiously weaving her webs, thought the world itself into existence.

"Spider Woman Stories: Legends of the Hopi Indians", G. M. Mullett

Base & Crown Energetics.

When the Base is integrated and sovereign, rooted in its
singularity, the Crown is empowered to form effective connections to everything. Once aware, we can easily choose to run
our energy like this, even if we are surrounded by people who
are running theirs the opposite way. We can remain sovereign,
with the Base complete and the Crown open, even when we are
challenged by others. We are gifted an advantage when our
Crown is open and interconnected with everything. We experience the whole truth. When we work the process of Prime
Healing we begin to experience that the world and our experiences are in duality. Experiences like confusion and clarity,
anxiety and openness, anger and focused clarity are part of the
same spectrum. It is simply a matter of opening the channel
within us and seeing the whole-truth for ourselves.

The value of this is immeasurable. Our experience of life
shifts. Everything is exactly as it should be. We can feel the love
and enduring truth of reality. This is the magnificence of the
Crown and the Base or in symbolic language the Sun and the
Cube.

With a sense of these two points, the Base and the
Crown, we can begin to understand why most humans are

blocked at the Base. Why have many individuals tried to manage the complexities of life with the Base blocked? Why would we try to deal with money, relationships, career, family and a myriad of other important areas of life through our Base? Why? Because, when we were born, our Primal Energetic System took over and we began a pattern of connecting our reactionary, survival-driven Base into the complexities of life as we encountered them. I personally never had anyone teach me to do otherwise. I didn't have a teacher or parent show me how to connect through the Crown, even though it is a far more effective and easeful way to function.

Most humans, from birth to about age 8, develop a behavioral pattern that utilizes the Primal Energetic Base to connect to their new world. This pattern is healthy when we are young, as the natural process of developing into a human utilizes Base Attachments to strongly connect to caregivers. We are an extension of our parents and family. I call this Primal Attachment because it is how we are able to grow our human bodies, minds and emotions with a model of guidance and support from our parents, caregivers and close relatives. But, just like our baby teeth, we outgrow the use of Base programing and need to shed the old ways of attaching in order to learn to connect through the crown.

For many humans the Base Attachment process is never shed. Many even believe that attachments and blocks at the Base is a practical way to navigate life. We begin to believe this is just how life is and that this is a game we need to play if we

want to win at life. Without the deeper awareness of how our energy naturally operates, we continue to pattern our connection to important areas of our lives with our Primal Energy in the Base running the show. For me, no matter how hard I tried, my world felt that it did not have a solid foundation and I was sure that if I didn't work hard all the time, my life was going to fall apart. In this reactionary state, with the Base open by being blocked, life is in a constant shifting struggle. We might even win the tug-of-war, we might get really good at it, but there is always stress and we struggle to keep our position. If we can make just enough money, get the right house, land an awesome job, or get the perfect relationship, then we can finally feel complete and enjoy life. But regardless of how well we tend to all these things, there's always an underlying anxiety that all of these things can be pulled away without a moment's notice. When we implement Prime Healing, the underlying anxiety dissipates and what is birthed is a sense of peace and steadiness that consistently illuminates our life.

Guided Meditation: Money

In this exercise, we are going to end some of the patterns of Base Attachments . Take a moment to get comfortable and take a deep breath. Allow yourself to relax a bit and allow yourself to feel the area just below you, down below your body. Feel the energy of the Base and now active the symbol of the

Cube. Notice how dense and heavy it is and notice if you feel anything attached to it. Feel your throne.

We will work with the energy of money. This is a simplified version of Prime Healing but you will start to get a sense of the process. This is one of the most common Base Attachments in modern society. Freeing ourselves from a Base Attachment to money provides us with a much more stable ease of being. Building a foundation on something ephemeral will not serve your happiness.

So take a moment to assess your Base by visualizing the cube. Feel all the dynamics of money: finances, taxes, savings, debts, desires, regrets, gains and losses. Notice the connection there and feel the tug-of-war with finances that automatically exists with anything that is attached at the Base .

Feel any fear, anxiety or tension relating to money at your Base. Attachments are simply blocks to unwanted experiences. Now it's time to feel and breathe these experiences and emotions relating to money back into the base.

Use Prime Breathing to breathe everything relating to money back into your base, reclaiming your inherent power back into the cube. Use the cube like a vacuum and now use the breath to simply breathe money back into the void of the cube. In in in.

Feel the entire concept of money drawn back into the base. Now bring it up through the body and from the center of the sun breathe money out form the center of the crown.

At the Crown, the radiant sun shining brightly above your head, the energetics of money are able to be worked within a much more enjoyable and effective way. Empowered by the reclamation of your own energy and the wisdom of your energetic centers, your connection to money becomes more clear, easeful and manageable. Repeat this process and get money in and up to your Crown.

Your Base is clear in its singularity, strong and stable. Your Crown is open and energized and while you can feel the complexities of money, you don't have to figure it out or have to know how money works. You can just enjoy that it comes and goes and there's lots of it out there. You know that you're going to use it for amazing things, that sometimes more will come and sometimes less, but you get to just enjoy that everything is as it should be with money. You can be amazed and be open to it happening like that.

At this moment, as you consciously experience the effects of Prime Healing, notice how it feels to be complete at the Base while open and connected at the Crown. When we connect to money from the Crown, we are no longer reactive to what money is doing. We don't feel pulled off-center when we lose or gain it, or find ourselves obsessed with maintaining, growing or defending it. Instead, our relationship with money is supported by our wisdom, power, emotional intelligence and physical presence. We can see the whole truth for ourselves, that money is both scary and exciting. We can allow ourselves

to be unblocked from any fears of money and sit on our sovereign Base and allow our crown to remain bright and open.

How does this feel for you? How does it feel to be connected with money from the Crown? If you need to stop reading and go through this process again, do that. Make sure you experience the connection to money in the Crown.

Explore this sensation and notice how re-navigating your connection to money, allowing it instead to reside at the Crown, allows the truth of money to unfold. Unclouded by anxiety and desperation, no longer a victim to money, you instead become an orchestrator of the universe of money. With this increased capacity of awareness, you are able to then connect to life in a more dynamic, real and complete way. Perhaps this simplified version of Prime Healing permanently changed your entire relationship with money, but I'm guessing for most it was just a little taste of how to work with the base and crown.

I know that for some people that the idea of sensing energy is new or even strange. I can assure you that the more you practice this process, the more it will start to make sense and become second nature. Energy Psychology is a tricky subject but I assure you, it will unfold and you will find clarity. I usually explain this material one-on-one, this book is here for many. For some of you, the pace is too fast and for some, it's likely too slow, my intention is to do my best to find the middle ground where you can follow. Remember, take your time with these ideas. Sit and breathe with the symbols and start to make your own journey with sovereignty.

To deepen the exercise, I'll offer myself here as an example. First I'm going to tune in and allow my Base to open, which I normally wouldn't do, because it's a waste of time and energy. But for the potency of this book, I'll cord my Base to money and down here in my Base, yes, I feel money. It's not comfortable, in fact, I'm cringing a little and with my Base opening as I'm sitting in my office in Nevada City, I begin to feel unsure of myself and increasingly insecure about my finances. I start thinking about the rent.

"Rent is coming, which is expensive and utilities have to be paid and there's all this expense I need to cover. I can get more money at work. Maybe I should work more. Or sublet one of these rooms. I don't really have a lot of savings. I'm traveling this month, so maybe I need to save instead of travel. How am I going to do this?"

So you can see that the formation of Base Attachments and blocks quickly paints a less than pretty picture. I can figure it out but it's a tug-of-war. It's uncomfortable, disempowering and unsettling. In a state of anxiety and fear, I'm apt to make some poor decisions. I'm likely to act out, create more problems and muddle up my life. That's not going to work for me. I've envisioned and experienced a much better state of being and it's time to return to it. So, now I'm going to switch.

"I decree in this moment that all Base Attachments and blocks to money are released and fully felt. I take money and all the fear and anxiety related to money into my Base and up

through my central channel into my Crown to allowing the whole truth be unveiled."

Ahhh, much better. In the Crown, I can feel the truth about money. I can feel that money is just a way for me to share and get things done. I can feel that there is plenty of money to share, that I'm meant to create Prime Healing and that I'll have ample money to do it all and it's going to figure itself out on its own. Money is both scary and depleting and exciting and energizing and I'm open to whatever experiences arise.

Ah, this feels so much better. Why would I not keep my connection to money in my Crown? Now I can use all of my energetic centers below it too, thereby giving me access to all of my power, wisdom and higher faculties. I don't create undue tension trying to block money but simply let things happen. Similarly, I don't worry about the trees growing or my blood pumping. It's not in my capacity to even fully understand how all of my cells work...but they all do. I don't understand everything about money, I can just trust that all is working exactly as it should.

Guided Meditation: Housing

Again return to the Base and tune into housing. Use two cycles of Prime breathing. See what cords are connecting into your Base in regards to housing, rent, or maybe your mortgage. Feel the attachments and fears at the Base going to rent, or the

bank, landlords, bills, or anything and everything to do with housing. Now, you can decree that these attachments and fears no longer serve you. The Primal Base is reactionary and it's always in a tug-of-war. It is not effective at managing housing. So release the attachments to housing.

When your ready breathe back all fears and unnecessary worry into the cube below you. Allow the energy to come up the central channel up into the Crown and you can feel housing in the Crown. You can feel like it's an adventure to find housing or take care of the one you have, to have the most amazing home and it's all figuring itself out for you. You feel secure from the one point of the Base and you can enjoy the amazing ride of life. By connecting to housing through the Crown, you can utilize all of your centers, emotions, mind, intuition, creativity, communication, thoughts, feelings, ..all of these can be utilized, all supported by a steady sovereign base. Connecting you through the Crown to everything you need to live your greatest adventure on planet Earth.

Are you beginning to see how Prime Healing works? These are simple examples but are showing you how the pattern works. The Base Attachments are released to provide a sovereign base of stability that is unaffected by outer phenomena. Your Base is your energetic grounding point. It's able to support you through everything and is unwavering in its stability and reliability. The only thing that is consistently needed to ensure that this point is unfailing is your intention to keep it clear of blocks. When the cords are retracted and the energy

that had been leaked out through them can be gathered back into the Base, a reservoir of energy begins to grow, providing a solid source for Crown to open. Now you get to decide for yourself. You decide if it is right for you. Maybe it's simply another viewpoint that inspires you to think more, or this can just be an enjoyable experience of reading another self-help book. Or perhaps you might say, "It does feel better to be sovereign at my Base. When I'm complete and sovereign at the Base and my Crown is open, it's a nicer, easier and more effective way to live." If this is you and you'd like to experience this chosen form of sovereignty and connection, keep reading.

Living Royally

Imagine the crown of a king or queen. It's lifted, raised up, the energy high and open. We wouldn't design a crown that's fallen inwards or closed. That would be like a helmet of someone going to war, someone who is controlled, taking orders from someone outside of themselves as a servant. The king and queen both have their crowns open and so do we. We can further envision the Crown above our heads emanating a sphere of brilliant white light, sitting above us like the radiant sun, with silver cords of connection naturally spreading from its luminosity. Crowned by divinity, trusting in life living royally, with grace, ease, with the ability to be present and appreciative of all that arises within and all around you. I like using the word "noble" to describe both the base and the crown. In the

common definition, it describes a high-quality person. If you say that something is a noble idea, goal, or action, you admire it because it is based on high moral principles. To be noble with our crowns held high.

The second meaning of noble can perfectly describe the Base. This comes from the scientific use for elements that do not react to others or this which resists chemical action does not corrode and is not easily attacked by other chemicals. Our noble base.

CHAPTER FOUR

Finding Your Rock

Is there a place in you that is sovereign? A place that is unaffected by this world and only for you? Is it in your mind, emotions or body? Answer this question again for yourself. Is there a place in you that is just for you? For me, when I had the experience in Las Vegas the answer was a clear yes and thus began the unfolding of Prime Healing.

If there is a place in us that is sovereign, then it is assumed that this place is not affected by anything in the world nor any person place or thing. Let's explore for a moment Einstein's theory of relativity, $E=mc^2$. If we do some basic algebra we can move mass (m) from the right to the left of the equation as Energy/mass=speed light^2 . In doing so we see that light and mass have a direct correlation to each other. Without complicating things we can deduce from Einstein's theory that mass or anything in the material world is light slowed down and conversely mass sped up becomes light. With the help of science we can also surmise that to be sovereign we would need to be able to affect light by either slowing it down or speeding it up.

This is the primary ability of the cube in the base of our energetic system. The cube is so dense that it is able to slow anything in the world including light. The deeper our consciousness goes into the cube the greater the density and at some point, everything is slowed down. Thus the cube at the base is unaffected by anything and in a state of sovereignty. Try this concept while you do Prime Breathing. See if you can sense the feeling of the cube slowing everything down like a black hole that is spacious and still.

Through Prime healing, we will become increasingly more aware of the system of energy within and around our bodies akin to the energetic system of the planet. It channels energy throughout our physical, mental and emotional bodies keeping us in harmony. It flows beyond our visible body into our energetic bodies. It is similar to the field around a magnet and can seem unreal unless we interact with it. While some people will see or feel these energetic bodies, we will be utilizing our senses beyond sight and touch to tune our conscious awareness into these energetic systems. I share this because you will be asked to get familiar and work with the base and top of your energetic system. Through the symbolic language of the cube and sun you will penetrate these areas and start to unlock your vast potential.

It's helpful to understand that animals operate from the Base. This is how herds of horses, swarms of bees and schools of fish move together so seamlessly. They act as one with the survival of one tied into the survival of all. It's a life of fight or

flight, being on alert, reaction and running. While this has its own magic and efficacy, we humans can choose to do something rather special. Unlike those in the animal kingdom, we can choose to be separate and unique and at the same time deeply connected. Living this way is easier and although it could potentially sound unbelievable at first, as it is practiced, it becomes a reference point from which to experience life. It's a system that supports us in a way in which everything we envision becomes possible. The decision one makes to close the Base is simple. That's just what I did in Vegas. I chose to have my Base complete unto itself, connected only to one point, my true self.

As you read this, you may even begin to feel your Base awakening and beginning to be more solid. Your conscious mind illuminates the possibility of sovereignty at your Base and your system responds. The opportunity at this moment is to become aware of your Base and more sensitive in your perception of it as you refine your ability to feel and interact with it. In the following chapters, we will use exercises, visualizations and breath-work to more deeply establish this awareness and connection.

Through the process of Prime Healing, you'll become adept at navigating the world through what we refer to as the Crown. In this way, we can connect to everything through the network of higher intelligence that brings us into harmonic resonance with life itself. As you begin to close up the Base and remove the blocks from it, the inverse automatically occurs in

the Crown. The attachments are transformed into connections. Like a battery, one side holds a positive charge and the other, a negative. The one terminal, the Base, becomes complete and independent unto itself. Depicted as a cube, the Base is complete and integral. If you can attune yourself to it, you'll begin to notice a feeling of sovereignty permeating your being and with that, a sense of trust that you are whole and complete in and of yourself.

At this point if I were sitting with you I would ask you, "How are you doing with feeling into the Base? How are you doing with the breathing? Is this simple technique starting to make sense?"

Here is a quick review- I know I'm repeating myself but it is this simple.

Prime Healing is similar to learning a new language, but way easier. The words in this language are symbols and there are only two, the cube at the Base and the small sun at the Crown. By picturing the black cube below you, you can work with this clear symbol that represents the absorbing all connections from this point to all people and concepts. By claiming the sovereignty of the Base, you will experience the unification and solidarity of the one thing that is just for you- your Base. When your Base's energy is consolidated to one steady point your crown can open and connect you to all of life.

If I was able to convey to you in one moment the immensely powerful shift of life experience that occurs when an adult is able to effectively close their Base, I could end the book

here. In order to effectively share this information in a way that makes this concept a reality for you, I want to offer you much more support. It's clear that it's important to share this method in a way that allows your mind, emotions, and body to incorporate this process in a way that evaporates your well-worn yet essentially outdated patterns. The rest of this book is provided as a manual of support to help you learn about the patterns of attachment and make the shift consistently.

Let's look at why most humans use the Base to connect with life. When we are born into our physical bodies, we do not have the faculties to operate on our own. Not fully developed, we are not yet equipped to connect to life through a sovereign and connected system. Could you imagine an infant or toddler being completely independent? No, of course not. In fact, without these Base Attachments, an infant would die pretty quickly. It is by being connected to a caretaker at the base that the baby is able to get nourishment and be protected. It makes sense that we would need to open and attach to our parent or child from our Base in order to ensure proper growth and development, even as a toddler and young child. This attachment is an essential part of human development and is healthy to stay running this way until a child is approximately eight years of age. In many traditions, ceremonies are held for a child at various ages that coincide with the release of Base Attachments. The child is encouraged and supported in their ability to connect to life in their own unique way and begin and to identify as themselves and not just an extension of their par-

ents. But for many modern cultures, there are no ceremonies, support or recognition of these transitions. As a result, the child is left corded into adulthood and throughout their lives. This idea of resolving blocks and attachments will be developed further in the chapter on the 4 ceremonies. For now, keep exploring with me the idea of going behind the scenes and seeing how our energy systems work.

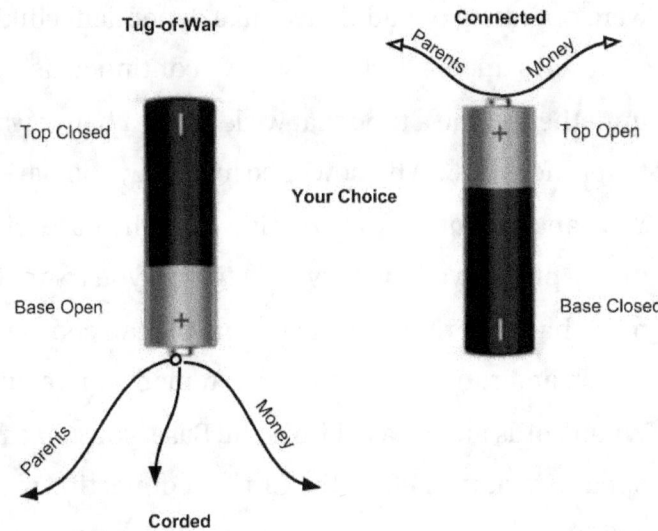

On the left of the diagram, the positive end is pointing down and it is open, representing what it is like to block the base and keep our hurt or fearful feelings away. The process of Prime Healing is the practice of flipping the system and on the right and shows how our system runs when the Base is sovereign and the Crown is open. Envision and tune into this happening within yourself. Imagine your top is open and your bat-

tery is flowing in the bottom and up and out the top. As we ex-
plained in Chapter 2, it's not that we were designed to run im-
properly, it's just that we didn't have the capacity at a young age
to be sovereign and it is now within our means to begin this
process. For some time, it was necessary for survival to be
corded at the Base, but we continued to survive and live like
this it becomes more apparent that our systems become
stressed and confused. We can now become cognizant that we
were operating our adult lives like dependent children.

It's understandable that we continued using this pattern
until there came a time that we learned a better way. For you,
that time is now. Why now? Because now, you have a choice.
You can continue to run your life from the Base with attachments pulling you in every direction as you try to fight life and
make bad experiences go away, or you can choose to flip the
switch and run your energetic system in a more fluid way.
When cords are released from the Base, you can ease-fully
open to beauty of life at the Crown, connecting with the world
with the power of your radiant sovereignty. We will get into the
concept of why the Crown and Base are mirror opposites of
each other, but for now just start to become more familiar with
the concept of having your Base closed and Crown open.

Witness your experience throughout the exercises and
notice the shift in your state of being not only during the meditations but during your day to day existence as well. Notice
your breath and how you feel in your body, the quality of your
thoughts and the shift in awareness you are experiencing. With

Prime Healing, you will develop a deeper awareness of your sense of wholeness and will become adept at guiding yourself back into a state of sovereignty as you develop your ability to navigate the ebb and flow of your life. When life brings you something new you will start experiencing it as something to be with, whether is is uncomfortable or pleasant.

The Practice of Prime Breathing

Now that you are learning the basic language of Prime Healing let's dive deeper into the breathing practices to give you a physical rather than just mental idea of how it works. Although we touched on Prime Breathing in Chapter 2, here we will get a more detailed description to deepen this practice.

As you will experience in this book some of this material is redundant. It's like learning a language with two words but they continue to have a deeper and deeper meaning. So as I repeat myself with the same words Base/Crown, Cube/Sun, Throne/Crown you can practice taking these two symbols deeper and deeper into your conscious and subconscious worlds. Introduction to Base Breathing.

The inhale is used for activating the Base. You can visualize the Base by using the cube symbol while drawing energy in with a long deep inhale into your Base. Remember to use the symbol of a black stone cube, dense, solid as your throne you are sitting on. The energy you draw in with your inhalation arrives from all six directions; up, down, right, left, in front of the

cube and behind. You can imagine it like a vacuum toward the center of the cube. Sucking everything in and because of it's immense density slowing everything down.

Sense the magnetism at the center of the cube that pulls everything into its center. Every cord to any person, situation and thing in this world is released as the Base draws everything into itself. Relax on the exhale. Take another longer inhale. Feel everything drawing into the cube below you. Feel the center of the cube drawing everything in as all attachments blocks are absorbed and slowed down. Relax on the exhale. Continue to take long inhales drawing in the energy from all directions into you. Attune to the sense that your Base is completely clear from all attachments as you do this.

Continue for another cycle, developing a good sense of how this feels. As you inhale, your breath draws the energy from all surrounding areas (below, right, left, front, back and top) arriving at the center of the cube. As you reach the end of

this long inhale, bring your awareness into the depth of the center of the cube. Exhale, relax and then repeat one more time. When you are done, you should feel your Base clear, strong and grounded, with your mind and body calm. Take a moment and feel the truth, you are a king or queen sitting on your sovereign throne.

Introduction to Crown Breathing

The exhale is used for the Crown. You can imagine a glowing sphere, a clear radiant white sun above your head. Visualize energy flowing from the center of the sun in all directions as you exhale. With each exhale, the energy shines out from the center of the sun and expands its luminous connection out of the sphere above your head, connecting to everything.

Feel the rays of the sun touching everything in the world: your every thought, your body, your emotions, every person, everything in the room. There is nothing that this sun does not shine on. Feel the center of the sun radiating and connecting to everything. Relax on the inhale and again exhale while transmitting the breath from the center of the sun to everything. Continue for another cycle to form a really clear sense of how this feels. Practice this breath and you will see how the symbol of the crown and the sun begin to come alive in you.

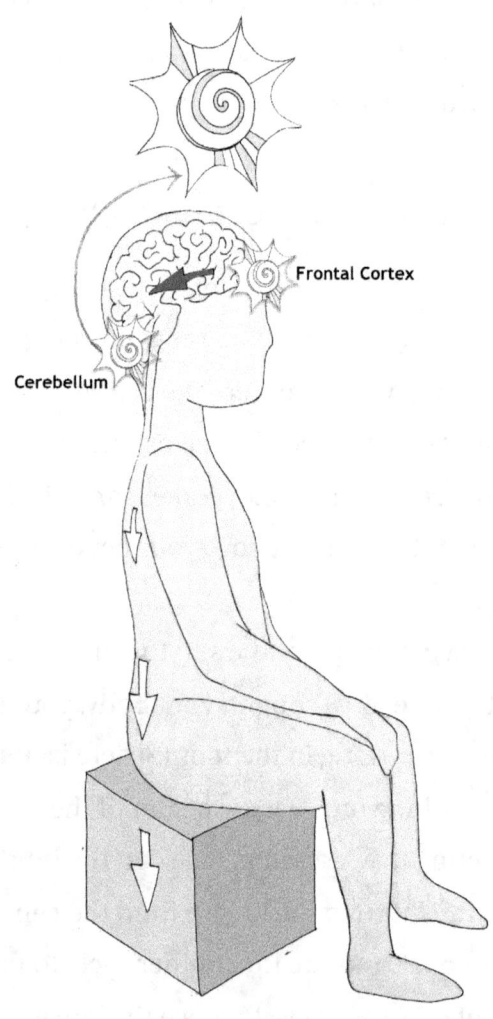

Frontal Cortex

Cerebellum

Solo Base Breathing

While learning Prime Healing and becoming familiar with how to keep your energy centers clear and activated, it is advisable to focus on the Base first. Do 3-5 breath cycles with just the Base. Find some time and a place where you can sit for a minute and focus inward. Laying in bed just before sleeping or when waking up is a great time. Or any time where you can turn the attention to the breath. If you do a meditation practice this will add a rocket boost to your practice.

Begin by focusing on the Base. You can amplify the practice by imagining the black cube below you and feel the density. Follow the steps for Base Breathing. Inhale slowly and feel energy streaming into the Base. Exhale and relax and prepare for the next deep slow inhale. The visualization should get progressively more vivid and with practice, you should feel the base solid and clear.

As you become more aware of your base energetics you might feel areas that are stuck or simply not flowing back to the base. This is the perfect time to ask yourself, "Why is this area still corded?" Sometimes people use attachments to stay safe or avoid feeling into tough feelings or situations.

Doing Solo Base Breathing will begin to reveal to yourself which areas of life are still blocked, those which you may have hidden from yourself, especially if abuse was present in childhood. You might have to spend time with that part of yourself before that part is ready to release the blocks and con-

nect. Continue the Base Solo Breathing until you sense that the energy is starting to really flow.

Solo Crown Breathing

Once you have formed a good connection to Base Breathing you can begin to do the same practice with the Crown. Keep it simple and do 3-5 breath cycles. If you want to do more that's fine, but 3-5 breaths is enough to activate the Crown. Similar to the Base Breathing practice, find a time when you can focus inward. At first, it will help to keep the eyes closed. Begin by focusing on the area about two feet above your head. Visualize a bright white sun above you. Follow the steps for Crown Breathing. Inhale and then exhale slowly, feel your energy and exhale, emanating out from the center of the sun above your head, radiating in all directions. Deeply inhale and relax and prepare for the next, more energetic exhale. On the next inhalation, relax into your own radiance, feeling and seeing the powerful sun that is your own light glowing above you. Exhale from the center of the sun outwards in all direc-tions. Continue this for a few more breaths.

If you are having any trouble with feeling the breath radiate from the center of the sun in all directions, it could be that the Base is blocked and open. These energetic centers function in a state of quantum entanglement, a phenomenon of resonance that quantum physicists have verified. Quantum entanglement links the properties of particles even when they

are separated by distances. According to research conducted by Professor Juan Yin and colleagues at the University of Science and Technology of China in Shanghai, the lower limit of the speed associated with entanglement dynamics is at least 10,000 times faster than light. How's that for instantaneous manifestation? What is happening to one center is also happening at the other. It is like trying to set sail and still being anchored to the shore. The more you push, the more resistance you will feel. So, if there is resistance in the Solo Crown breathing, don't push and strain yourself. Simply notice and return to Solo Base Breathing and continue to work with that portion of the Prime Healing processes. When the anchors of Base Attachments are lifted, Solo Crown breathing will be effortless. If you notice you are challenged in any particular area, take note and feel into it. The more information, insight, and awareness you have about this particular Base Attachment will provide you with the power to effectively dissolve contracts when we reach that part of the process.

Prime Breathing Exercise

After some time, Solo Base and Solo Crown Breathing will become easy and natural. It will amplify the work you are doing and keep you humming all day long. When you have the Solo Breathing down, you are ready for Prime Breathing. I know you did this briefly at the beginning of the book but now it's time to take the symbols in deep and really feel your throne

and crown. Not only will Prime Breathing allow the Base to stay clear and give the Crown the power to connect, but this clear energy will also begin to resonate throughout the body. This is similar to what the Taoists call the Microcosmic Orbit, an ancient practice of circulating energy around the body using the breath.

Prime Breathing is a combination of Base and Crown Breathing. It can be done anytime, but when you are beginning, it's best to find a space where you can focus inward with your eyes closed. The practice only takes about 1-2 minutes.

Begin by finding a time that you can focus inward. Eyes can be closed or open. You can be laying down or sitting however you like. Activate the visualization of the black cube below and the white sun above. On the first inhalation, begin Base Breathing. Draw the energy in the Base with a long easy inhale. As you begin to exhale, let your awareness travel up through the vertical channel traversing the center of the body. It should travel quite quickly up to the Crown to the center of the sun. The remainder of the out-breath will radiate from the center of the sun-crown outward. Near the end of the exhale, let your awareness travel around and down to about two to three feet from below your butt. As the next deep inhalation begins, again draw the energy from every direction into the cube and again, as the exhalation starts, quickly bring awareness up the center of the spine and out the top of the head to the center of the sun and radiate the light outwards in every direction and again, near the end of the breath, guide your awareness back down

and around the outside of your body and then as you inhale, draw the energy back into the cube-throne. Continue for a few more breaths.

It can be help to use your hands to follow the breath during prime breathing. Use the hands to follow the breath into the base, move the hands up and track the breath as you exhale out of the crown. There is a video available at Prime-Healing.org.

When you are done breathing, enjoy the clarity, harmony, and vitality that Prime Breathing brings. Sit or lie still for a moment and feel your sovereign throne and crown radiate. At first, the mind could wander and it's possible to lose the connection to the Base and Crown. When you continue to use Solo Breathing while deepening your connection to your Prime Centers and you immerse yourself in the practice of the Four Ceremonies (chapter 10) while empowering your "I Am" statement and Mudra (later as well), you will begin to feel more and more power and ease in Prime Breathing. After some time of Prime Breathing, the sensations of the Base and Crown will stay with you longer and longer. It should come to be that you look forward to this practice like a hot cup of coffee or a beautiful sunset.

Prime Breathing Easy Steps

- Start by relaxing and turning your awareness inward.

- Inhale into the Base.

- Exhale from the Center of the Crown Sun in all directions.

- Inhale into the Base.

- Exhale from the Sun Crown in all directions.

- Repeat at a comfortable pace.

- End by letting the breath relax and being aware of the Base and Crown at the same time.

As you make this practice your own, you can use Prime Breathing with your eyes open anywhere you choose. You can be sitting in a noisy restaurant with your family and friends and take 1 or 2 breaths and feel how much more solid and present you are when you can tune yourself anywhere at any time. When a musician is getting ready to play, they take the time to make sure that their instrument is perfectly tuned. Similarly, we can use Prime Breathing to tune our human-spirit instrument and be in harmony with ourselves, others and our environment anytime, anywhere.

Prime Breathing with Hands

To help facilitate the awareness of connecting our breath to the Base and moving it through the Crown you will use your hands to follow the breath.

You can use Prime Breathing Hands in a sitting, lying or standing posture.

Begin with a long relaxed inhale. Have your hands follow your breath in towards the cube. At the end of the inhale pretend like your hands are holding the Cube. Now move your hands up the center of the body as you begin to exhale. Have the hands trace lines from the center of your Crown outward and up with the exhale. Let the arms fully extend and the palms face out. At the end of the exhale slowly continue to move the arms out and back down. When the hands get about waist level you should begin the next inhale into the Base. Continue this process for a few rounds.

Start with a Slow Inhale
Imagine Holding the Cube

Begin a long Exhale as
Hands move up to Crown

Exhale out of the Crown
Imagine Light going out in every direction

Finish Exhaling
Hands extend out and float down

Repeat Three Times

For the video go to: PrimeHealing.org

This breathing practice is essential for Prime Healing.

When Prime Breathing becomes second nature, you can sit for an extended period of time and do many cycles. The transitions of the breath through the circular pattern will become more refined and captivating. The breath will lengthen and become smooth and slow. Your sense of timelessness and

deep inner stillness will increase and the process will feel like it moves on its own. Your connection to the symbol of the cube at the Base and the sun at the Crown will become more vivid and alive for you. When even our childhood fears are embraced, when we no longer cord to our lovers or family and the world, then the breath will flow. We will be able to be present to emotions and experiences that we might have blocked and now have the presence to be and breathe with them as the arise.

In this state we can enjoy the miracle of simply being ourselves. We can sit and watch the flow into our Base and rise up into our Crown with the ease of our breath. Residing in the natural state of sovereignty accepting all that life brings us as part of our journey.

CHAPTER FIVE

The Whole Truth

When we invoke the image of the cube and establish our sovereign base we are able to see life from a new perspective. Good and bad become part of a bigger flow through our open system. As we sit on our ever still base we see that everything is in service to us experiencing life and from this throne we are able to see that all parts serve us.

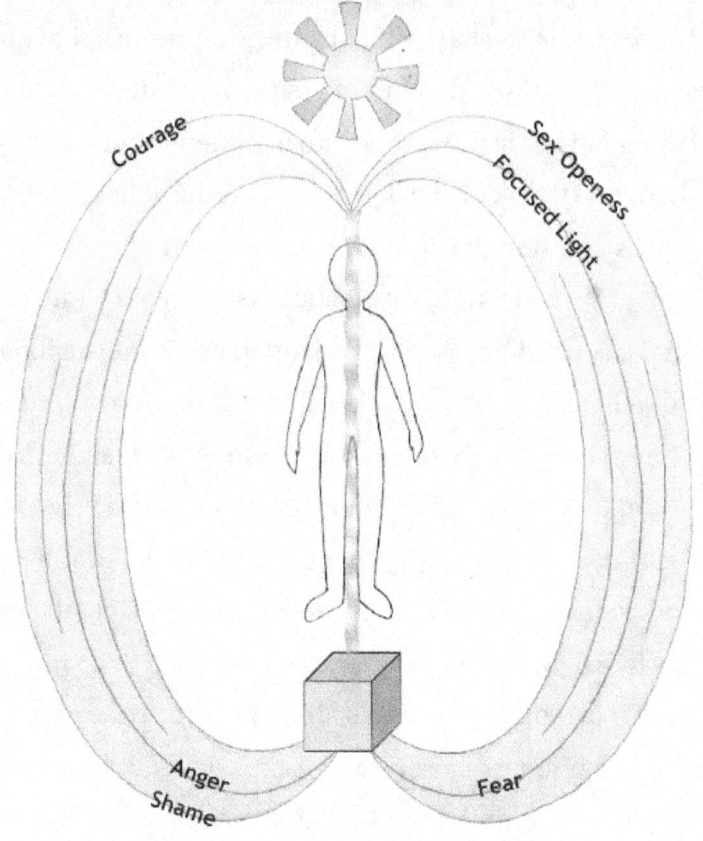

A client that exemplifies the ability to see the power of having a sovereign base was Shelly. Shelly had a full life. She ran her own clothing line, had a 4-year-old boy, a 2-year-old girl and traveled often. She was in serious overload and anxiety when we first started working together. In our first session, she learned how to use the symbol of the cube and the sun and was able for the first time in many years to feel at peace. We then went through the 4 ceremonies and were able to stabilize her base. She did great for the first 5 days. She said that she felt in rhythm with her kids and her life and felt joy returning to her life. Then she had a fight with her husband and everything started to unravel. Instead of sitting like a sovereign queen she started panicking that her old patterns of anxiety had returned. Instead of using the symbols to experience her power she used them to try to get rid of her pain. This amplified her base blocks and sent her spinning out of control.

When I saw her next she was in a state of high anxiety. She described how she was trying to use Prime healing to get rid of her fears. I coached her that this doesn't get rid of fears it just enables us to become stable enough to feel them fully. We began to explore her fear of being alone and saw how this was the root of her fights with her partner. We did Prime Breathing and got her back on her throne. From this place, she explored her fear of being alone. She cried as she felt deep into this fear. As this fear opened she was able to use the base to draw this fear of aloneness back into herself. As she let this fear open she began to relax and describe that as she breathed this fear in

and up to her crown that at the center was a lake. She said that the lake was deep calmness. We both sat for some time as she felt deep into this calmness. An image of her being alone and calm by a lake filled her with relaxation. As she continued another round of prime breathing she could feel in the Crown that being with others was exciting and stimulating and being alone isn't lonely but was calming. Sitting on her base with the crown open she could see both sides of the story. Aloneness and being with others coincided with calmness and stimulation. For so many years she felt that being alone was terrifying and was equal to death. As she let go of blocks at her base Shelly was able to see through her childhood fears and allow the deep truth to permeate her consciousness. She committed to getting a babysitter at least once during the next week and going to sit by a lake near her house. I look forward to seeing her soon.

We can see that when guided to be on her sovereign throne, Shelly was able to unlock the truth of her loneliness. By unblocking the loneliness and allowing it to flow through her system she was able to see the loneliness had in it deep calmness. This is a key principal of Prime Healing: everything has within it its opposite. The cube has the sun. Fear has courage. Hate has love. By taking the first step and enacting a sovereign base we have the ability to see the whole truth. Sometimes it is challenging to stay on our throne when faced with moments like rejection. But when we can, we can experience that even rejection has within it the seed of connection.

I'd like you to have the opportunity to experience for yourself how seemingly opposite experiences can be supporting, creating and nesting in one another. In this following experience, I hope to invoke both a nervous sensation and a joyful sensation at the same time. With practice, you can feel how deep nervousness supports the open joy and wow of life.

Whole Truth Meditation

Find a comfortable place to settle yourself. Begin by taking a long relaxing breath. Breath into your Base and now out through the center of your Crown. Now imagine a large heavy stone...a large, dense and heavy stone. Now envision the stone being dropped into the ocean and sinking through the water. The heavy stone falling and falling, but never hitting the bottom. The stone continues to fall and fall and fall, falling endlessly through the infinite water. Dense, heavy and sinking, the stone continues to fall through an endless ocean, with water all around it in every direction. As you visualize this stone, allow yourself to evoke and embody the feelings that would naturally arise when falling forever through an expanse of water. Stay with the nervous feeling that will arise in the stomach and also sense deeper into the joy and freedom of the endless unknown. Falling and falling through endless water but never hitting the bottom, forever. Notice all your feelings, maybe an uneasy feeling arises, perhaps even a feeling of aloneness may surface as you witness the stone falling through the water with

no bottom. Continue to allow yourself to experience this feeling, this feeling of one focused point of density, with no connection to solid earth. Go deeper into the feeling in the stomach and allow yourself to fully allow anything that arises as you tune into this isolating and endless feeling of the stone falling through the water forever.

Play with the simple visualization on your own. It will get you familiar with the idea of trusting the duality of life. It will enable you with your Throne and Crown to trust that everything in life is a part of your kingdom.

Eve is another student of Prime Healing that demonstrates how freeing the blocks in our base allows us to see the whole truth. Eve is a 21-year-old dancer who started working with me because she was stuck in her career and personal life. There was so much confusion in Eve's world. She, like most, had the pattern of connecting at the Base. She was in a tug-of-war with her career, with her parents who didn't want her to be a dancer, with money and the challenges she had supporting herself as an artist and even with dance itself by judging herself against other dancers. As our first session progressed, she took the red pill and decided it was worth taking a chance to close her Base and connect instead through the energies of her Crown. We worked by slowly feeling into the blocks she had with her mom and dad. She was finally able to see that she was blocking the places of judgment and rejection in herself and thus keeping her base blocked. Eve saw how she spent most of

her energy trying to avoid these feelings and trained endlessly to avoid these experiences. By accepting her parent's fears and judgments as her own she was able to draw them into her base. With tears in her eyes, she felt her own acceptance of the places in her that are judgmental and saw from her throne that inside, the judgment held the seeds of true acceptance.

She knew that dance was her true path and that her friends and community did support her work and if they didn't, she could handle that feedback. From that point, so many changes transpired. She was offered many opportunities to perform and teach and she felt clear. It was amazing to watch her flip. When her light came on, it was so big that it filled up the room with such a radiant brilliance that I referred to her as "The Sun Dragon." Her shift from a timid, unsure and power-less being to a shining Sun Dragon, a confident creator of her dreams, was a testament to the potency of Prime Healing. She had started the first session feeling so muddled and confused, but she caught up in a hurry, going from feeling scared and small to feeling the truth of her being, beaming her light, em-powered and excited about life. The next time she came in, the change was so dramatic, it was like being with a completely different person. She sat in front of me in clarity of presence. She told me, "I get it...and I'm living my life like this." She was taught techniques that helped her in the process of clearing contracts and was instructed in the utilization of mantra and mudras. She used the mantra, "I am the Sun Dragon," and paired it with her own unique kinetic mudra that anchored it in

for her. Once she had cleared all of her contracts and had prac‑ticed the mudra with the "I Am" mantra and continued to tune her energetic system with Prime Breathing, she was able to maintain a sovereign state. It only made sense to her that her Base was just for her and connecting was better and more clear at the Crown. Life felt freer and more easeful and she noticed her external environment was granting her opportunities for her true expression of purpose. She felt a calling to work with younger women to help them embrace their own judgments and rejection and with the tool of dance see how judgment and acceptance, rejection and love are part of the same connected flow. With the tools to anchor the process, it's been easy for her to maintain this state and live a life that she feels she was born to live.

Duality

"Duality: the quality or state of having two different or opposite parts or elements ." Webster Dictionary

Understanding duality in ourselves is the key to unlock‑ing our blocks in Prime Healing. When we are able to prepare ourselves with breathing and knowledge is comes like a big ah‑ha! " My life is empty and meaningless and also full and pur‑poseful! At the same time."

The symbols of the Cube and Sun let us define the po‑larities of our dualistic nature and see that it present in every aspect of creation. Night/ Day, Hot/ Cold, Good/Bad.

We become polarized when we only want to see one side of duality. " I only want to be seen and see myself as confident and relaxed." The pressure is enormous and leads towards deep anxiety. Instead seeing that shyness and confidence ebb and flow between each other. And when we are accepting both realities without blocks we can flown between them according to what is most attune with our environment.

Duality and all your issues are on different sides of the same coin. Good/ Bad , Yes/ No. With Prime Healing it becomes easier to be with whatever aspect of you or life shows up. What is true? Are you good or bad? Yes, you are both. Staying in that sweet neutral non-dualistic place as the coin of life is flipping in front of you. Open to whatever shows up.

" Thank you duality for showing yourself to me."

Once you decide and discover for yourself that it's easier to live with a clear unified Base and an open Crown, it becomes a path of continually infolding how to live as a King or Queen. It does take a certain level of trust and a clear direction to have this happen but once you've decided to unblock your Base and declare your Base as complete, it is that way. It follows your directive, because your Base is yours.

As you sit with your book, take a deep breath and allow your body to relax. We are going to go through a simple decree, something you can follow, change and make your own in any way you want. I will give you an example of what it is like to command the Base. First, take two full Prime healing Breaths. In the Base and out the Crown. Now begin to read and repeat the following statement:

"At this moment, I decree my Base as Sovereign. I decree that my Base is only for me, that nothing, no person or situation, has control over my Base. Only I do (deep breath). I decree in this moment that all attachments and blocks from my Base are now within my awareness and will begin the process of unveiling themselves through the Base and into my Crown. All past contracts are now released. I see clearly that safety does not come from Base Attachments, blocking or cording to others, but from being sovereign and in full connection to everything in my world. All the deep and scary emotions and nightmares that reside in me are welcome and felt. As these are felt and drawn into my Base, I bring these energies through my central channel and out of my

Crown and experience the Whole Truth. I see that fear and love, light and dark and all duality are within me as by Base and Crown are mirrors of this truth. I decree that all attachments and blocks to money, relationships, and all other things are now absorbed and slowed down by my magnificent Throne and connect to everything through my radiant Crown. I decree my Base is precious and the one thing I keep only for myself. It is what allows me to be me. By having my Base clear, I can feel steadiness that I am a King - Queen on my throne and all this is remembered by simply breathing.-

Complete with 2 cycles of Prime Breathing with Hands.

Now sit and feel for yourself what it feels like, your Base below you, sovereign and still. As you feel this embodiment of peaceful radiance, notice the connections you've created at the Crown and notice the fullness that comes with choosing connection to occur this way. Notice the calm strength and sense of trust that permeates your existence when all the questions and complexities of life are left up to the mystery of life. Feel how relaxing it is to have a steady clear base that is not affected by anything.

CHAPTER SIX

A Story from the Beginning

"It is better to travel well than to arrive." -BUDDHA

Now that we're getting deeper into the Prime Healing process, I would like to share some stories with you from my adventures through life that has helped shaped me and this work. I'll take you all the way back to 1999. That year always reminds me of Prince's song, 1999. He was sure that you might as well party because time was up. I was only twenty-two and life was really just beginning. I had left my old life in New York when I discovered that all roads lead to Venice Beach and was living in a little oceanfront apartment with my first real girl-friend, Emily. Life was wide open. I was training at the best yoga studio in Venice, surfing and working as a gardener. I was doing pretty well but struggles with money and my girlfriend were beginning to stress me out. I didn't know about Base blocks back then but could feel the weight of life tugging me and pulling me down. It got to a point when I found myself fighting with my girlfriend about the littlest things. What was I

doing wrong!? I was just barely able to keep myself from freaking out. I had left my old life in New York to feel free and alive and I remember sitting on the balcony of our apartment feeling trapped and lost. I decided that I was going to leave. This was the opposite of what I set out to find. I talked with Emily over the next week and after much yelling and crying, we agreed that it was over. I told her that I was going to go back to Maui for a while. In a strange turn of events, she ended up coming with me. Camping with her for two weeks was a deep process, all the while both of us knowing we were soon separating. The day before she left, we decided to only say the Hawaiian phrase, "Me ke aloha oe ike ike po." This translates roughly as "With our love, we have power in the darkness". We had said everything to each other over the past two years and both of our hearts were hurting deeply. We didn't have enough presence in our thrones to handle embracing the reflections of each others pain and blocks.

When the day came to take Emily to the airport, I decided to give her all of my money and bank cards to help her make the transition. I watched the sweetest thing in my life fly away. Then I walked back to Paia town and just sat. My heart hurt and I felt like everything I had done just left me more muddled, confused and hurt. My Base was so corded and attached I couldn't tell what had made me so defeated and lost. I didn't know if it was Emily, money, me or something else. I just knew the only way to begin to figure this out was to get rid of everything. For the next 6 months, I stayed in Maui and didn't

have or use money, not a dime. I know it is hard to imagine how I ate and lived, but each day had its own way of working out.

I decided that all the effort I put into getting money, had just left me more confused, so I decided to abstain from any interactions with it. It was my first real ceremony. Well, it actually felt like two ceremonies. In retrospect, disconnecting from Emily was my 13-year-old ceremony and relinquishing my ties to money was my 18-year-old ceremony. (I will share more about what I'm referring to in chapter 10.)

Life has a funny way of working out. Sure there were days where I had some freak-outs when I would get hungry or I had to deal with an infection on my foot. But, after months of not using money it started to get more clear. It was my presence and connection to the moment that created my experiences and without money, my base was much more unblocked and stable. Of course, money makes some things in life happen quicker but it also masked the fact that money had been ruling my life via my Base Attachments. Prime Healing would have moved this process quicker, but I didn't have the tools I have now and I was young so I pushed through it the hard way. I didn't have the language for it back then, but my Base was starting to feel free.

I was emailing with a friend in Bali and she invited me to come to stay with her and her friends there. "Hmm, I guess it's possible to fly to Bali but the no money thing might be a bit of a challenge," I considered. I went to the public library to use

their computer to research tickets. I couldn't believe it. I had found out that round trip tickets from Maui to Bali were only 240 bucks. The SARS outbreak was just ramping up and planes were flying half-empty that went through Taiwan to Bali. I sent an email to Emily and asked if there was anything left in my account. She got back to me and said, "Yes, you've still got $240." The synchronicity was not lost on me. This was making sense. She said she had started a good job and was living back with her parents so she didn't need it. I had her buy my ticket and off I went. I remember the strangest feeling when I was on the plane. It was that feeling of the stone falling through water forever. With my Base steady I could feel the discomfort and excitement of traveling into the unknown with no money or plans and at that same time at ease with the joy of falling through the ocean forever. I felt something falling away and something new arising in its place. My system was steady and getting used to being sovereign and open.

Bali was similar to Maui, only easier. The people I was staying with were wealthy and we lived like royalty. They loved the fact that I didn't use money and were beyond generous to me over the next two months. They were spiritual and open people. We went on adventures and ate great food and had dance parties by the pool. Nevertheless, I grew restless in Bali and decided to travel. These friends couldn't believe I was choosing to leave my opulent life, leaping ahead with no money into the unknown again. I packed my little backpack and got a ride to the shipping port in Bali. For the next 2 weeks, I trav-

eled by boat, hitched rides and walked all through the Indonesian Islands. That feeling of the stone falling forever grew. Every day was an adventure and I met so many people. I sometimes went without food and sometimes ate too much. There were times when I got stuck in the rain and others when I was able to relax into the luxury of a beautiful yacht headed to the next amazing island. By remaining present and trusting throughout the journey, it became evident to me when I was getting stuck and when I was connecting. It was like a switch. When my Base was clear and my Crown was open it was easy to flow in my experience. I didn't know the symbolic language of Prime Healing but it was there all the same.

A moment that stands out to me was after traveling for over a month by boat, motorcycles and buses through endless Indonesian islands is when I arrived in Singapore. I was in the Southern port enjoying the sights of this incredibly clean and organized new place. I went up to an information desk and asked if they spoke English. He lifted his eyes to meet mine and said, "Of course, English is my first language." I felt immediately at ease. It was going to be such easy travel here. I wouldn't have to use charades to communicate. I asked him how I could travel across Singapore. I also explained that I didn't have or use money. This guy, in his perfect suit, looked like I had just punched him in the gut. Completely insulted, he said, " You are not allowed to be in our country if you have no money!' He said that he was going to call the immigration officers. Completely perplexed, I took a step back and explained that I have traveled

the world with no money and that most people are kind and enjoy helping me on my way. He said that in Singapore to have no money is a very bad thing. He said that even the poorest people in Singapore have jobs and some money. He was insistent that I was screwed and that I was either going to jail or I would be immediately kicked out of the country. He looked so official in his suit that he had me believing this story. I could feel my Base getting shaky and blocking my own feelings of insecurity and fear. Instead of trying to convince him of anything, I backed away and sat back down on the bench. The feeling of my Base came back and I decided that the worst they could do would be to kick me out of the country, which would be a free ride to somewhere, which at the moment seemed better than here.

A dapper looking Singapore man in a sharp dark blue business suit approached me and asked what was going on. I told him how I was traveling through Singapore and the guy at the service desk was angry that I didn't have money. He sat and we talked for a while. He explained to me that in Singapore's culture, money is a very important part of the modern culture and that it is threatening and even scary to hear that someone has no money. It would be assumed that they would be in grave danger without money. I told him that I was focused on being clear of energetic imbalances in my life and I had chosen not to use money because I didn't want money or anything else to have rulership over me. He was really amazed that I was sitting there with no plan, no money and no way out. He left and

thanked me for sharing my story. After a few moments, the service guy approached me. I thought he was going to have me kicked out of the country but instead, he handed me an embossed black envelope. He said it was from the gentleman who had been talking to me earlier. Inside was a bus ticket! The service agent showed me to my bus. When I boarded the bus and I was taken back. Usually, these big tour buses had something like 80 seats. This bus had about 12 seats in their own little sections, with privacy curtains. The attendant took me to my seat, put my bag away for me and explained that whatever food or drink I wanted would be brought to me. Oh, luxury. After two weeks of being on foot and packed into more cars and little boats than I could count, this super plush chair was like heaven. I spent the next two days sleeping, watching movies and eating shrimp, coconuts and ice cream as Singapore, Malaysia and Thailand came and went from my view.

I found my way into temples and all sorts of amazing places after arriving in Northern Thailand. After a few months and a set of adventures that will have to be saved for another time. I eventually decided that I was going to fly back to Maui and then to Los Angeles. Although life was raw, I recognized how quickly it responds when my base is clear and my Crown is connected to my environment. I was ready to use money again and be more active in society. I saved up enough money working at a restaurant in Chiangmai Thailand and performing through a talent agency to fly back to Bali and then make my way to Maui and finally Los Angeles.

I arrived in Venice Beach near sunset and sat on the sand reflecting on my adventures. I felt clearer than I ever had. I was still young on the journey but I was beginning to understand the difference between blocking and connecting. As the sun was setting over the Pacific Ocean, I recall thinking that I was ready to use money. I concluded that if I was going to live in a city, I couldn't go collecting food from trees. As I was thinking this, I noticed something in the breaking waves pushing up on the sand. I walked over and picked up a big wrinkled melon. I sat on the beach and dug my fingers into the green soft flesh. To my amazement, it was a perfectly ripe honeydew melon.

CHAPTER SEVEN

As Above So Below

So now that you are becoming familiar with the Prime Healing process and see how the Base and Crown are inherently connected, we will take this a step deeper into the concept of them being mirror inverses of one another. Like the saying goes, " As above, so below." When one center opens the other closes. When the Base is dark, the Crown is light. When one is isolated, the other is connected. These two primary points in our energetic body, one above our heads and the other just below our seats, are the foundation of our energetic system and when properly functioning, are our key to being connected to ourselves and the world.

By now, you've most likely experienced a moment that exemplifies why it feels better to live with the Base sovereign connected to one, only for you, without any attachments to other people or things.

You've experienced the ease when the Crown is open and connecting us to the world. When your Base is sovereign, all the energy that was lost in attachments returns as inspiration. When the Crown is joyously connected to everything and

an individual is filled with the radiance of divinity that is always there to claim and enjoy, life feels amazing and much, much easier. We experience a harmonic connection to the array of complexities of life.

Imagine a queen sitting on her throne in her opulent throne room. See her in her royal gown with a golden crown atop her head, ruling over a beautiful land that is her domain. The crown's points are directed upwards and raised to the sky, adorned with precious gems. You can see her energetic Crown glowing above her head. Her Base like her throne is clear, solid, unmoving and complete. She is confident, secure and at peace. She knows herself in her entirety, safe in her wholeness, identified completely in deep knowing as the queen. She knows who she is. No one and nothing can say or determine otherwise, nothing can pull her off-center and she has no contracts or cords that could supersede the sovereignty of self this queen so gracefully enjoys. She is sitting in full connection to her fear, insecurities, and doubts and is allowing them to bring her to higher heights of courage, security and knowing. Through her Crown, you can see she is connected to her advisers, her family and all of her people, fully aware of all that transpires in her realm.

Conversely, imagine the queen sitting on her throne while her Base is attached to a plethora of things that exist in her queendom. You can imagine the sovereignty and serenity previously enjoyed would be severely challenged. Every adviser, every person in her realm and every point of attention that

arises in a land such as this pulling her at her Base. Let's say the Queen's mom walks in and because there are still blocks at the base she becomes nervous and doesn't want to feel this or be seen as not in control.

Instead sitting on her sovereign throne, the Queen has to hide her irritation with her mom, fearful of her judgment and being exposed she has to block this experience. The tug-of-war would be constant, tiresome, likely debilitating the Queen. When a Queen is functioning as a Queen she already knows and is with her deepest fears and highest power. The point is for us to experience the awesome feeling of sovereignty that a Queen or King experiences as a ruler of their own domain.

Any area of life can be experienced in its fullness when connected to the Crown through the Base. If it's money. You can be at peace with the idea that money is depleting and scary and in the same breath an exciting adventure. You can trust both sides of the story. When your unblocked your sovereign throne can take care of you.

After learning Prime Healing, I realized that every client that had hired me as a healthcare practitioner, coach, teacher or therapist was blocked to experiencing some aspects of life at the Base. It was easy enough to recognize their Base Attachments as they explained the tug-of-war drama in their lives relating to any one of their issues. They were experiencing monumental problems caught in a loop of self-imposed fears. When the system of Prime Healing revealed itself to me it was like a clear path that allowed them to get realigned with a simple idea that we are whole. They got to experience the underlying truth of all situations when connected to them from their Crown. All of these daunting and insufferable 'problems' instantly became the wonders of being a human.

Iris is a 62-year-old accountant who came to me seeking help with general anxiety. Although she claimed a big part of her anxiety came from worrying about the financial futures of her two children, both of whom were in their early twenties, it became clear that her real worry was about her own financial future. How interesting that someone who had worked in finance for over thirty years, had savings for retirement, who

owned her own home and by simple analysis, was financially stable, was worrying so much about money.

During our session, she told me that she chose to be an accountant because her Chinese immigrant parents felt that it was the only way for her to be safe and successful. In this simple statement, I could see so much through the lens of Prime Healing. She had not released attachments to her parents and let their fears become her fears and blocked them with all her power and now she was perpetuating the propagation of these blocks and fears to her children.

Because of the attachments, no matter her effort with finances, the Base was in a tug-of-war with money and many other areas. Even though she put in great effort to master money, the underlying blocks to her parents' fears were beginning to take its toll. She said that she could not imagine retiring and that all her effort to become financially stable would be lost it she stopped working.

First, I explained to her the concepts of the Base and Crown and described how these primary points dictated how she interacted with life. I drew the chart of a stick figure with a square at the Base and a circle at the Crown and showed her how these centers worked for young children and how they transformed for a sovereign adult. These concepts made sense to her but when I asked her if she was ready to release money from the Base and bring it to the Crown, she froze.

She explained to me that after a lifetime of reinforcing her attachment to money, it felt scary to let it go. It felt like her parents would disapprove and something terrible would happen. So we slowed the session down and I had her go through the exercise of Prime Breathing. After settling into the breath, I guided her through a meditation to release some smaller fears like social anxiety from her Base. After she could feel the process, I then took out a dollar and had her release this one dollar from her Base and connect it to her Crown. We then spent the next 20 minutes going through the 4 ceremonies and it was clear we could go deeper into her attachments to blocking her fears about money. She took the first step and was able to open her Base energy and draw fear back in. As the connection rose to her Crown, it was palpable even as a witness that she was deep in the connection. In a calm and slow voice with her eyes closed, she explained that she could see that this deep fear was in her family for a long time. She could sense that deep in the fear in something that looked like a green and black blob with teeth was a shining light. That in her crown she could see that the shining light was true freedom. An unbreakable, radiant freedom. Freedom from slavery, oppressive governments, and poverty that had plagued her family for generations. She was terrified to look into this fear, but now that she had she could see that it was her gift to bring to the world. She explained how she was going to continue to open this fear and share this with her daughters.

We made a 2-week plan so that she could continue to release the attachments to money and feel the freedom and wisdom in the choice to connect to money with the Crown. She then went on to explain that she wants to help others connect to the deeper truth behind the fear of money. She said that this might be her retirement transition and was really looking forward to sharing her wisdom with others.

Life is a dynamic process of living, dying, sleeping, waking, inhaling, exhaling, having money, not having money, problems, no problems, endings, beginnings... all of this is life.

Crown Meditation

Let's practice a meditation together to activate the circuit of the Base to the Crown. Bring yourself into a comfortable position. As we begin, tune into your Base. Experience the energy of your Base in its unified singularity and feel the Crown open in its connection to life. In this state, we are going to go through a few different categories.

Bring your awareness to people in your life and allow your Base to open to them. Don't worry, once you know Prime Healing, this can be reversed in an instant. Feel the tug-of-war. Feel the wavering and imbalance, the reactionary state that arises and the sense of discomfort that is evoked when we are attached at the Base. Now, command your Base to release all of these cords, any contracts that have been made at the Base with you to be dissolved and for your Base energy to be avail-

able to you only. Deepen into that for a moment and draw all the energy that was connected at the Base to come back. As you release all connections to others, breathe the energy back to the Base. As the energy returns to the Base, exhale and send the connection to everyone through the Crown. Expand your awareness to envision the shining sphere of light above your head, connected with white radiating light to all of those you're connected to in life. Feel into your mother, your father, and your first caretakers. Thank them, regardless of your previous or current relationship with them, for giving you and support-ing your life in any way that they have, in all ways, big or small. Thank them for being born and allowing you to be born and to live. Feel connected to them in the Crown.

Connect to all past and current partners, lovers, friends, kids, ancestors, teachers and allies and offer appreciation and gratitude for each and every one of them. Feel the gratitude ex-pand, filling you with radiant light, in deep appreciation for all beings in the world. Feel that everything was and is exactly as it is meant to be. Come back to the Base, feel it as one and feel the Crown connected to everyone.

Through the process of full feeling and releasing blocks to others and absorbing them back into the Base we are able to remain sovereign from them. Simultaneously when we are clear at the Base we are able to make deep connections to oth-ers through the Crown.

CHAPTER EIGHT

Journey To Hawaii

In the middle of writing this book. I decided to take a short trip by myself to Maui to sit with all this information about Prime Healing that was pouring through me. Working with clients, I was seeing incredible transformations and felt the ease and power of Prime Healing at work. I just didn't want to present anything that wasn't true for me. Writing a book on energy psychology is not an easy task and I wanted to be sure that all aspects of Prime Healing rang true. As we will see in book two of this series, when we live our destiny we also embrace our shadow. For me, the shadow of presenting the truth comes with being fake. So off to Maui to see what is fake and what is real.

Fresh off the plane, I took my rental car and drove right to the top of Haleakala Volcano Crater. At over 10,000 feet in the center of the Pacific Ocean, Haleakala crater is one of the quietest and clearest places I know. I found a rock cropping at the top of the crater offered a ti leaf and crystal to the mountain and sat for a few hours. I practiced my "I Am" statement and Mudra began Prime Healing Breathing and felt my Base be-

come very still. As this stillness deepened, my Crown opened to the massive beauty around me. I was introducing the science of Prime Healing to the island. I asked if there were glaring holes or fake shortcuts in Prime Healing. I asked earnestly and listened. Nature is such a clear teacher when we slow down, listen and wait. I could feel my Base and Crown in harmony. My breath started to naturally breathe in with awareness at the Base and breathe out through the Crown. For the next few hours, I sat breathing in the Base and out the Crown. My mind became deeply relaxed as it began to bridge into the subconscious world using the symbol of the cube and felt my solid throne below me.

It felt like a dream to be sitting on the volcano. What a gift this was for my life and a gift to be able to share. As I looked down below me, I saw clouds were rolling into the crater. I asked the volcano and the island if they approved of what I was doing with Prime Healing. In the exact place, I was looking down upon, a circular rainbow formed in the front of the clouds. I'd never seen a perfectly circular rainbow, especially from above. Looking into that circular rainbow, I felt inspired to commit to just one name for the process. I played with many names but looking into that rainbow I said in a calm clear voice, "Prime Healing." I felt that I had received a clear answer from nature and myself on the potency and truthfulness of Prime Healing. So now I was ready to go swim and explore Maui. I went to waterfalls, ocean caves, bamboo forests and all of my favorite beaches. Every place I went, I let Prime Healing

take me on a journey. So simple. With the newfound breathing to accompany the symbols to connect me to my Base and Crown, I would slip into meditations. It felt like I was tuning myself like an instrument. Once the top and bottom of the instrument were tuned, through the process of a few breaths, everything else would fall into place.

Near the end of my Maui trip, I was sitting under a shady tree near the ocean on the North Shore at Baldwin Beach. As I looked up, a dear friend of mine was walking by. His name is Harold H. Bloomfield, MD and goes by "Hare". He is an eminent Yale-trained psychiatrist, a leading psychological educator, and a bestselling author. I spent a good part of the afternoon walking and talking with him about life and especially about Prime Healing. After showing him the process, he turned to me and put his hands on my shoulders. With his bright smiling eyes said that it was time I brought this to the world.

I sat back under my shady spot in the sand and allowed my breath to tune me. Joy rushed through me as I felt Hare's words lighting up the consciousness within me. It was my final confirmation about Prime Healing and it made my path ahead feel very clear. Although I was not an author at the time, I committed to sharing this with you.

As I was leaving Maui, I felt complete with my mission to be 100% sure and committed to the Prime Healing process. As I was going through the TSA security line at the Maui airport I looked up and saw this statue and felt yet another confirmation.

This towering sculpture is in the courtyard outside Kahului International Airport by local Maui artist, Shige Yamada.

CHAPTER NINE

Contracts

With the basic understanding that it is the combination of the process of birth and the time between the ages of 0-7 years, that act as the catalyst for the creation of what we call Primal Coding. We can begin to unravel this basic programming or Base Attachments. Attachment does not have a positive connotation because they are held in place by blocks and stunts the fullness of life experiences. Attachment means that we are tethered to something and whether its money, relationships, or health, by attaching, we are caught in a tug-of-war. This has been the reality for many, including myself.

By now, you've begun to feel the difference when you exercise the ability to breathe in the Base and open the Crown. Through the meditations and the previous chapters, we've been able to offer an awareness of how this process is self-created and can be maintained as the on-and-off switch of life simply by directing the connection to flip from the Base to the Crown. With a still base, you can sense your attachment to avoiding certain experiences and release them by accepting the

pain that you have blocked and keep your energetic circuits open and flexible.

The human condition is interesting because we need to make a contract with our parents and the world that we will fully cord to the world in order to begin a life here. To ensure you would be nourished, protected and fed, loved and cared for and have your needs met, you needed to attach to your mother, father, and surroundings. This is a natural and healthy process that should be a stabilizing process for a child from zero to eight or so. There is a point of transition when a child can be guided to release attachments at the Base and conversely begin the stage where they can connect in the Crown. Coming-of-age ceremonies are present in many in indigenous cultures. In Australian Aboriginal society, a Walkabout is a rite of passage during which males undergo a journey during adolescence between the ages of 10 to 16. They live in the wilderness for a period as long as six months to make the spiritual transition into adulthood. You can begin to see through the lens of Prime Healing that this would allow them to develop their clear connection to self as they un-cord from parents and tribal members.

Without a clear transition from the early attachment patterning, most people continue to live a life of attachment to life instead of connection. As we begin to cultivate romantic relationships, the pattern of attachment continues because it's the only way we know. It's not so much a conscious choice to attach, it's an automatic reaction based on childhood patterns.

I have worked with many married couples for example, and it's amazing to see similar patterns come up after they have been together for several years. The woman complains that the man isn't providing enough energy and the man coun- ters that he doesn't know what to give to her anymore and that nothing he does is right. So they engage in the constant tug-of- war of relationship. Regardless of how much they focus on fix- ing the things that come up, the tug-of-war continues and the connection between them suffers. Even with the best inten- tions to support, nurture and love each other, with ingrained patterns of attachment and fear to feel hurt places within themselves, they end up fighting and hurting each other. To some degree, we see that this struggle is rooted in contracts they both have made and agreed to hold consciously or sub- consciously. It is the agreement to attach to each others' Bases and protect themselves from pain that keeps the patterns in place. These contracts operate within the system of Primal Coding and while in place, make the shift to sovereignty rather difficult if not impossible. Until we clear the contracts and un- block all potential experiences, the Primal Coding continues to receive commands from the subconscious to regain control of the energetic system, especially when some type of trigger presents itself.

We see that when the Primal Coding is active, the Base automatically attaches to a situation, usually out of fear of a negative experiences. For example, with the Primal Coding running, people instinctively attach their base into money.

Even if they have enough money, there continues to be a fear of the possibility of running out of money. Unable to relax when they have it and terrified when they lose it, they always feel imbalanced with money. The Base Attachments and the contracts and patterns are now becoming self-evident. Now we are going to help you become more aware of how these attachments work in different areas of your life. You will begin to build the ability to very easily un-cord the Base, bring the Base to one, bring the element of life that was corded to the Base up into the Crown and connect to it.

Through this process, you can ask yourself about any aspect of life. By evoking the relationship or situation and asking yourself, "Am I connected in the Crown, or am I attached at the Base?" You will be able to effectively evaluate how you are relating to each area of your life. Again, it's like a light switch. If you are corded at the Base, you will feel reactionary and stuck in that area of your life. If you are connected to the crown, you will feel lighter and more able to navigate.

To discover where we are attached, we can start by going through the following list. While this a general Top 8 List, there are many more possibilities that may be unique to you. Let's begin by going through this list. As you read each item take a moment to breathe at least once in the Base and out the Crown. Take note how the different elements feel in the Base and the Crown. * Yes, feel free to write anywhere in this book.

Feel Into	Comment	Comment
Mom	Base-	Crown-
Dad	Base-	Crown-
Partner	Base-	Crown-
Friends	Base-	Crown-
Work	Base-	Crown-
Money	Base-	Crown-
Home	Base-	Crown-
Body	Base-	Crown-

Go back through the list and observe what you wrote about each subject. It will start to bring to your awareness the areas that are blocked at the Base and those that are flowing in and up uninhibited. It is by experiencing the "negative" aspects that will allow them to be breathed into the base and unite with the whole truth in the crown.

Decree

Next we will learn how to use the Prime Healing process with a Decree. Using a decree sets the stage for us to then go deeper into our attachments and unblock any holdings in our system by feeling the fullness of the block.

This is an example of how to make a Decree. It will begin to release old programming that don't serve you. Fill in this contract by choosing an area of life from the previous list or you can choose a unique one of your own.

Prepare with a round of Prime Breathing. In and Out.

Decree

"I Decree that my Base is only for me. My Base and all attachments are released as I accept all the blocks that have kept them in place and allow them to be breathed back in. In this moment, I release all attachments, blocks and fears to _____ and fully feel all the past and present hurt emotions or thoughts that have kept this stuck in me. -
I now use my breath to connect _____ in my Crown. (Take a deep breath into the Base and breathe out the Crown). I allow all blocks from this issue to be fully felt absorbed into my Base and to rise up into my Crown as I experience the fullness of this connection in my Crown. I am grateful for _____ as it allows me to become more of who I truly am."

Take some time to really work through some items on the list above. I suggest at the very least to go through the process with money and parents. You'll find the more you go

through the process, the more you can reside in a balanced and harmonious state. You can use your hands for Prime Breathing to amplify the experience and really feel the energy in both the Base and the Crown.

When I do Prime Healing with clients the easy part is to activate the Base and Crown, the tricky part is to sit with the emotions and thought patterns behind the blocks. In writing this book I am aware that this will be the focus of the next book. This is what modern therapists call 'shadow work'. I like the practice of the Buddhist call Chod. The gist is similar to shadow work, the importance of knowing and managing the ugly, shameful parts of the self and acknowledging rather than ignoring them. A nice intro to the practice of chod is the book, " Feeding Your Demons" by <u>Tsultrim Allione</u>.

Sit with your deepest fears and trust that inside are the seeds of your heaven.

If you prefer and are inspired to rewrite the contract in your own words, go for it. Also feel free to rip the page with the Decree out of the book and keep it where you can see it, or take a photo with your phone and print it. If there is an area of life that isn't on the list that you feel called to work with, this is encouraged as well. This is provided as a guideline and example and as you work the process, it will become clear how to best to create something more powerful and personal that works perfectly for you. At some point, all the words will be resonating in one symbol, your sovereign cube.

As the attachment is released by accepting the pain that you have blocked, you may become aware of other ones, even ones not listed here, that call for your attention. Each time you go through this process and clear another category of attachment, you will feel the results.

Feel the base supporting you with unwavering support. You can visualize with greater ease and depth the base symbol of the dark cube, strong ,balanced and sovereign. From that place of sovereignty with the Base supporting you, feel the Crown open and sit with the feeling of connection in the aspect of life you just worked on through this process. Sit with that feeling and notice any differences in the way you experience relating to it. How does it feel? You may want to jot down some notes or write about the shift in your journal as you witness the results of changing the way in which you choose to connect to these important areas in your life. The experience should be enjoyable and you may just wish to feel it fully and allow that to be your preferred way of being with the process. Some choose to do a daily meditation and if this feels good to you go for it. In this state, life becomes more of a flow than a fight. Decisions become easier to make, problems are solved more quickly, challenges are easily overcome, discord settles into peace with grace and ease.

I invite you to choose a way to work this process that feels enjoyable. In the next chapter, you will learn some tools to anchor this process deeper. When I work with clients, I explain that this isn't meant to be a discipline. It's something you

should feel good doing, drawn naturally to do it when the time feels right and above all else, it should work. You may find yourself naturally drawn to go sit in the sun on a bench that looks comfortable on your lunch hour. Recalling some things that came up at work, you might find yourself called to go through this process by simply focusing on how you are running your energy in relation to your boss and coworkers. Then rewiring the contracts with this process. You can do it while you are driving to work, while you are taking a shower, cooking breakfast, swimming laps, exercising or relaxing on your couch. Just like a light switch, you'll notice the more you practice, the easier it is to access the place of peace with a single breath. When the switch has turned the light on at the Crown and the cords have released from the Base, life becomes a lot easier and we finally get to experience what it feels like to enjoy life in the flow.

CHAPTER TEN

The Four Ceremonies

Stages of Attachment

When is it healthy to have Base Attachments? Let's begin by looking at the stages of development that occur in early childhood. This is the phase of life that I call, "Primal Coding". It's during this time period from birth through age 7 that we healthfully cord from the Base. We do not have the faculties in these early years to be independent. It ensures survival and safety and is absolutely necessary in order for a child to grow, thrive and connect. When a baby is not provided the opportunity or ability to cord properly at this early stages of life, we see developmental and emotional issues arise. Children are not able to get what they need and if they survive, they often have deeply seeded issues that stay with them into adulthood and throughout life.

Let's look at the stages of life in relation to the process of attachment. During the time from 0-3 months, often called the third trimester, humans continue development outside of the

womb. Because humans have such a large head to hold advanced brains, we are born before our brains are fully developed. At birth, the infant is vulnerable to the world, without the capacity to feed, protect, move, guide, or care for itself. Without consistent connection, nurturing and protection, an infant can not thrive. By attaching at this time, unspoken needs are felt by the parent at a primal level and the dynamic between them is strongly corded. At this point, it's necessary for parents and caregivers to do everything for the young one: carrying, feeding, changing, bathing, nurturing, protecting...all needs, wants and desires are attended to by the caregiver. It makes sense during this time for the parent to open their own Base up to the child as well. The developmental period that spans the seven years following birth is very important. During this time, a child is not equipped to command their sovereignty and connect to life this way through their Crown. The healthy attachment supports the bonding between the parent and child, offering a sense of safety and belonging that's conducive in the formative years. As children grow and reach the ages of 4-6, the child begins to widen their scope of connection. They cord themselves to teachers, friends, pets, siblings and other aspects of their life as their way of interfacing with the world around them.

You can begin to see through this process why they are attachments in our base in the first place. But it is also within these natural attachments that the seeds of blocks form. It is from this lens that we can see that this is why, for example,

many people have issues with their parents, even if at a subtle level. Because while our base is attached we take on others and the world's pain as our own. When we are hurt during this time we usually do not take it as a deep experience to feel fully but rather the hurt feelings as something to be avoided or blocked. I know this can seem complicated but understanding the origins of our blocks helps in releasing them. It's actually simple all you need to do is feel and breathe in the cube and trust.

Stage 1- Age 8 , Parents

When the child reaches approximately 8-years-old, the development of their Base Attachments reaches a pinnacle of completion. At this point, a phase begins in which the child begins to slow down the development of new attachments and is ready for the first steps toward sovereignty. As the new operating system becomes more integrated, the child experiences themselves and the world around them in a new way. At 8 years, the child is now ready to withdraw their attachments to their parents from the Base and begin unfolding the awareness that they are connected directly to life through their newly opening Crown. Instead of attaching with their parents through their Base, their new sense of self and sovereignty encourages them to look beyond their parents for the source of life. Enjoying growing independence, these children begin to enjoy later bedtimes, sleepovers at friends' homes, new responsibilities, hobbies, sports, artistic expression, deepening

friendships and most importantly themselves. As they age, their Base begins to become more complete as the cords gradually diminish and their ability to connect through the Crown is enhanced.

If you have 0 issues with either of your parents and were loved and cared for in every moment in the exact perfect way, this will be a snap. But for 99.99% of us, there will be blocks accepting the flaws and pain of our parents as our own. But when we do this, we simultaneously realize the great gifts our parents and the world has given us. A seed of truth inside our blocks, that we picked the perfect path to unfold our greatest dreams.

Stage 2- Puberty, People

Shortly after puberty (age varies), marks the start of the second ceremony. It's during this phase that the attachments to friends and society begin to release from the Base. Now they can choose instead to connect through the Crown, their relationships become deeper, freer and more enjoyable. Eventually, they come to realize they are distinctly separate from each other and at the same time connected. As attractions, relationships and social connections are created, these resulting experiences provide an opportunity for growth and evolution. As one progresses with the second ceremonial stage, they learn to be more clear with their own identity and at ease connecting to others.

Stage 3 - Age 18, Material World

At age 18, the third major transition occurs. Although attachments have been in the process of dissolving, cords do still exist. Life becomes more complicated. The young adult begins to drive and school becomes more demanding. They may start working and making money and could find themselves drawn to a particular kind of career or life path. While their awareness certainly grows as they are introduced to the concepts of money, career, politics, philosophy, society, religion and new belief systems, teens aren't fully developed in their ability to self-govern at this point. Lacking total ability to manage these areas of life, they draw on the experience and safety of their families, teachers, and mentors, maintaining the cords connecting them to those that help them manage these areas of life. Being underdeveloped, it's natural for them to keep attachments at the Base, but as we know, keeping these cords intact comes at a cost. They will experience a lot of tugging from the push and pull that comes with having cords at the Base and at some point, usually around the age of 18, the young adult begins to consciously choose how best to connect with the complexities of life. Attachments are traded for connection and as life progresses, awareness, sovereignty, and discernment grows.

120

Stage 4 - Age 21, Body & Earth

Between the ages of 18-21, this process evolves and by the age of approximately 21, the development into adulthood reaches completion.

At this stage of development, attachments to the body and to Earth can be released. Because the body has transcended puberty and reached adulthood the full sovereign base can be developed. Leaving all the fluctuating hormones, aches and pains of puberty behind, the body can instead be connected with the higher wisdom and awareness engendered by the Crown, providing the newly matured young adult a greater clarity of themselves and their own body.

For complete sovereignty at the base the person also begins to be independent from earth. When this information came to me I was somewhat surprised. But after releasing the connection from earth at my Base I was able to draw this connection in and up and see the fullness of this connection in the Crown.

The Four Ceremonies

Now that we've explained the four stages of healthy attachment, you've become more acutely aware of how the process of full attachment between the ages of 0-7 evolves into an ebb and flow of attachment and connection until early adulthood. At this stage, a sense of personal sovereignty can be enjoyed in a new way. We are complex creatures and often

leave these developmental attachment and connection processes unfinished unless a person becomes aware of these attachments and chooses to complete the process consciously.

With these four ceremonies, we can complete the
process of releasing attachment and absolve blocks that might
be holding them in place and strengthen our sovereignty at our
current age by traveling back in time to this age. To begin these
ceremonies you first need to activate your throne and crown
with Prime Breathing. Breathe in the symbol of the cube at the
base and breathe out the symbol of the sun at the crown. You're
likely getting the hang of it by now. In, Out.

Ceremony 1: Parents

As you read, begin to relax and activate Prime breathing. Next, tune into your inner world and find yourself at eight
years of age. Recall something you liked to do at age 8. Perhaps
you can recall your birthday party, your classroom or bedroom,
or maybe a dance recital or sports event. See yourself as your
eight-year-old self and notice the way you look, how you feel
and tune into the way your experienced life at this age. Intro-
duce yourself to your younger self. Be with them and feel your
eight-year-old self with you now and have them sit in front of
you facing you. Explain to them that it was natural to connect
with your parents in a deep way at the Base as part of the proper growth necessary to reach this stage in life. It made sense
and at this point, it's no longer necessary. Share with your child

self that it is possible to connect through the Crown and with that comes a whole new level of living life. Share that this is done by releasing the Base Attachments that you'd used to connect with your parents. Show your younger self how to draw back the cords, close the holes in the Base and pull the energy up into the Crown. Invite your eight-year-old self to draw both parents one at a time into the base and then up to the crown. Enjoy the feeling of connecting with your parents through the luminous Crown and share in the happiness that this rite of passage gifts you both. You can both sense how natural and essential this process is on the journey towards harmonious connection and embodied awareness that is supported by the grace and ease of sovereignty. If there was abuse, neglect or trauma, there could be fear that wants to keep cords in place. With compassion and gentle attention, assure and guide your younger self in a way that feels natural and easeful. Spend some time together and when it feels right, close the ceremony with loving acknowledgment and appreciation for one another and this beautiful experience together. It may be that this ceremony needs to be repeated as the child self becomes more trusting of the process. Find time to become quiet and spend time with your eight-year-old. With your loving kindness and attention, this ceremony provides the opportunity to complete this potent stage of self-development. With your guidance and assurance, the child within is guided into letting go of fear and as the cords release and dissolve, a deep sense of safety takes its place.

Ceremony 2: Social & Sexual

Again activate your base with Prime breathing. Then, bring yourself to the time when you had just passed puberty. See yourself and listen to your voice at this age. Remember something you liked to do at this age. Ask the young one to sit to your left facing you. Notice your clothing, energy, body language, sense of self and purpose. Honor your younger self for reaching this new level of maturity and celebrate the blossoming of this newly emerging sexuality. Tune into your connection and share the insight that along with this rite of passage comes the opportunity to become more complete. Share in the awareness that up until now, you've been connecting with friends, schoolmates, teammates, crushes, boyfriends, girlfriends, teachers, counselors, coaches and siblings through the active cords you've created and sustained at your Base. Take some time to guide this teen version of yourself through the process of noticing how these cords are connecting to others. Go through each important relationship and guide your younger self into breathing these connections back into the base, spending even more time clearing all of these cords to those with whom you feel a special attraction. As your guidance illuminates a new way of residing in the Base, free of cords, with all its energy available only for yourself, show this young self how to instead choose to connect with all of these people through the Crown. This will take many ceremonies to

clear all connections but slowly breathe each relationship back into the Base and up into the Crown. With your guidance, your younger self will be able to enjoy friendships, romantic attractions, choice, individuality and self-expression in a much more secure and embodied way. This is so powerful for the post-pubescent self and this work has the inherent potential to very simply, yet very deeply, rewire programming, particularly in romantic relationships. You are now able to foster deep loving connected relationships with a strong sense of self.

Ceremony 3: Life Path & The Material World

Again center yourself and access your sovereign throne with Prime breathing. Now, bring your awareness to yourself at age 18. Perhaps this is after high school or the first year of college. Envision your face and body, hairstyle, expression, and clothing. Recall something you liked to do around the age of 18. Ask the 18-year-old to sit to your right facing you.

Become aware of all the cords that are still connecting to life through the Base. Tune into your thoughts and feelings, goals, aspirations, dreams and fears. Sense how you are experiencing life with all of its peaks and valleys, responsibilities, commitments, plans and surprises. Notice how you feel in relationship with survival, success, and self-responsibility. Bring into your awareness the concept of money. Invite your 18-year-old self to dissolve the cords to money and offer assurance that by connecting to money through the Crown, money becomes

much easier to navigate. By connecting with this complex sub-ject at the Crown, higher wisdom can be utilized to create prosperity, invest wisely and engage in the arena of financial abundance in a much clearer and stable way. Witness how money had been pulling at the Base, making career, finance, success and much of life feel like a push and pull. Realize how this is essentially a very unstable way to relate to money. Though it's normal for teens to cord to money, a new milestone has been met at the age of 18 and these cords are ready to be released too. Explain that by dissolving these cords at the Base, life will feel much more easeful. Life purpose, career, college, and big choices about path and future are also best navigated through the Crown. By rerouting the way we connect, all the faculties of the human system can be activated to support a more complete way of living. Inviting a deeper sense of safety, security, wholeness, trust, self-awareness, acceptance and cel-ebration of life, even when it surprises us and things don't go as planned. Gifted with the ability to experience the self with greater awareness and to express oneself as an activated indi-vidual, beautiful and completely unique, life becomes mythic and we bring to it the cultivated capacity to really enjoy this adventure we call living.

One by one, go through each of the following life ele-ments having your 18-year-old breathe each in and up to the Crown. Use your hands and teach the 18-year-old how to breathe them in and up.

- Money

- Rent
- Clothing
- Buying Food
- All Material Things
- Cars
- Life Purpose

Continue to visit this former version of yourself regularly, cultivating trust as the cords are released and the Crown continues to activate new connections, assuring them through the process that this work is laying the groundwork for an amazing life.

Ceremony 4: Body & Earth

Again center yourself with Prime breathing. Now, connect with yourself at the age of twenty-one. Remember something you liked to do around this age. See yourself and feel what it was like to do the thing you liked doing at 21. Now ask the 21-year-old to behind you facing you. Notice any cords that are existing at the Base, particularly in relation to the physical body. Experience and feel this Base cords and when you're ready, activate the symbol of the cube and feel your base breathe them back in. When you feel these connections to the body come back in pause and lift them through the body to the Crown. Notice how the connection to the body feels in the Crown. Your height, weight, skin, hair, health, agility, strength, appearance...all is exactly as it should be. In full acceptance

and appreciation, notice how this evolved perception shifts the experience. Invite this 21-year-old self to engage with the body through the Crown and when health or body issues arise, they can be connected in a way that becomes informative instead of worrisome. Next, ask the 21-year-old to feel their connection to Earth. Feel how up to this point the connection is in the Base. Begin Prime Breathing and allow the connection to Earth to come back into the Base, travel up the central channel of the body with a pause and breathe out the Crown. Basking in the connection to the ocean, land, trees, animals and all parts of the Earth through the Crown.

Each of these ceremonies is best met with consistent and careful attention. You will enjoy great benefits by spending some focused time with a sincere emotional connection as you go through the ceremony again with each of these younger selves. Each of these ceremonies will present you with a much more evolved and secure sense of self. You will enjoy growing stability in the Base and you'll experience a more profound sense of connection with the inner infinite self. Just as you helped them start the work, these younger selves evolve with you as time goes on. Your 8, 13, 18 and 21-year-old selves will all be doing the work with you, complete with you, as you, connecting with the wholeness of life. The ceremony continues in every moment and the attunement you enjoy ripples into the infinite timeless evolution of your true self. When you feel this process is complete, you'll find these ceremonies have sta-

bilized your own ability to work with your Base and your Crown and be able to handle any situation life brings to you.

The most important and potent ceremony is the present moment and by focusing on what is present in your awareness, you are able to invite all of these younger selves into your current experience.

Homework: The Circle of the Four Ceremonies

After you have done the Four Ceremonies, you can perform the Four Ceremony Circle on your own. Find a time to sit where you can be comfortable closing your eyes for 5 to 10 minutes undisturbed. As you sit, use Prime Breathing to activate your Base and Crown. Then imagine sitting in front of you is your 8 year-old self. See the Crown, small but growing. Be aware of the newly established freedom from old base attachments to parents. Keep practicing Prime Breathing and feel your own Base clear and Crown open.

To your left, see your post-pubescent self (13 or whichever age is appropriate for you). Notice their Crown has grown larger than the 8-year-olds. Feel their new freedom from society and sexuality. Feel this in yourself as well. Take a long Prime Breath and feel the Crown open.

To your right, see your 18-year-old facing you. Clear all attachments to money, life purpose, school and any complexities of life. As well, feel that their Crown is much larger now, radiating and connecting.

Behind you, feel your 21-year-old self. Sense their Crown and your Crown. Feel the Crown expanding, full and open, like the sun rising for the first time. Clear and bright. Free from attachments even to the body and Earth. In its place, a deep connection to everything.

Feel them all looking at you. Let them see all of you. Let them feel how powerful they have become as you radiate and connect to all of life. Take a moment to close the circle by thanking each of them. As you close the circle by breathing everything back into the Base, feel them shining in you.

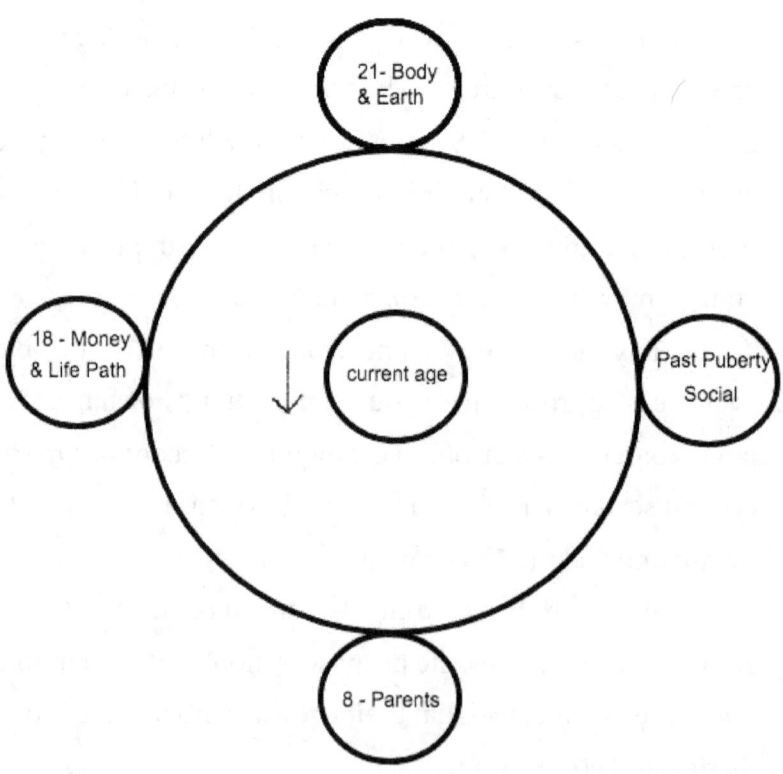

PRIME HEALING

As you complete your work, they complete their work. As you help them start their work, you set the right tone for them. As you support them in their process, the benefits reach you where you are now. You can tell them with clarity and conviction that you will continue the work they've been doing with them. As this work is practiced, it becomes even more second nature. You'll find as things come up, you'll naturally attune to them through the sovereign base and open Crown.

CHAPTER ELEVEN

Parents and Children

It brings ease and a deeper understanding of the phases of raising a child when we understand the Prime Healing process and how it relates to parenting. Many parents can go through periods of feeling deeply overwhelmed. Parents are overwhelmed with the responsibility and amount of energy it takes to be the primary source of care for a child. We are offering a consistent base cord to our child and in some ways, this lessens the amount of time and energy we have for ourselves. It is only overwhelming when this is done unconsciously. When a parent is aware they are opening their Base and providing secure attachments to their child, it is done as an offering of love.

Bringing balance to life as parents is done by using the principles of Prime Healing. When we have the skills of connecting through the Crown, we can strengthen these upper connections even while the Base is partially corded to the child. Deep levels of harmony can be achieved when a parent actively takes steps to keep the Base clear and connect through the Crown with one another and conversely let their relation-

ship stay polarized and loving. As parents, we also have the unique opportunity to become masters of Base and Crown energies and support the healthy and strong development of our children by providing secure attachment to their own healthy system. I suggest that parents find time at least once per week to take time without their child for at least 3 hours. During this time you can go for a walk in nature or just turn off the phone and find a quiet place to be. You can also sit and go through the steps of Prime Healing and the 4 ceremonies. I suggest the practice of "I am" statements and the decree. Parents should also write a new decree that includes opening their Base to their child. During these weekly parent retreats as a mom, dad or primary caregiver, we can release all attachments. You can also enjoy the inspiration and surge of energy as we fully open our Crown. Take the full three hours and get creative. Journal, dance or find a way to allow yourself to embody being independent and open. At the end of the time, open the particular area of the Base that is best suited to cord with the child and feel this deep connection, strong and revitalized. You may be amazed at the response from the child as the connection is clear and vital.

Keep in mind that this attachment is strongest from 0-3 years. At about 4 years of age, primary caregivers can create longer breaks from the child to actively release the base cords. At around 8 years, parents can do a ceremony to release the attachment completely. Of course, this is replaced by Crown connection that they will enjoy with their children for life. A

deep sense of love, respect and trust can resonate in this life-long relationship.

As parents we experience a boost in our lives as we fully embrace our sovereign selves again. When our children reach 8, since we have the experience of attachment and releasing while raising the child we can find greater harmony with ourselves and the world. Once fluid at working with Prime Healing, we can also practice deepening the attachment to the child when needed. By directing the Base with the breath through Prime Breathing, we can feed energy to the child's Base connection. If we have multiple kids, this becomes a fantastic opportunity to feel the difference between our attachments to each child at different ages and stages, naturally reflected in the child's needs. Conversely, an adept Prime Healing practitioner can take even a few Prime Breaths while doing the dishes and release the cord to the children and with one breath, reconnect. We can find unique ways of playing with this fluid process. While parenting we can also dive deeper into the Four Ceremonies and clear all other unnecessary Base attachments. It is more essential than ever that we only cord with our children keeping the rest of the Base clear.

With some effort, as parents we gain mastery of our Prime Centers by offering our life force to our children. Instead of being overwhelmed, we become flexible and clear within our system. When the time comes to un-cord from our child, they will be propelled into their lives with more focus, clarity, and joy.

CHAPTER TWELVE

Onward into PRIME HEALING

Working as a high school teacher and behavioral thera-pist, I came to the realization that when we are working on changing patterns, we need to establish new ones. The Prime Healing process makes it very easy to create new patterns even if the old patterns have been running for decades. By activating our Base and connecting instead through the Crown, we can immediately experience the cessation of the old pattern in fa-vor of one that works better for us.

To activate this process at this moment, we are going to go through another quick visualization to strengthen the Base and Crown. Yes, this is the same meditation over and over. It's simple but you bring in deep insight by going deeper within yourself.

Guided Meditation

Sit comfortably. Bring your awareness to the space be-low your seat. Here, at the Base, we envision the heavy cube, black and solid. As you connect into the experience of the en-

ergy at the Base, you may begin to really feel the enormous weight of the cube. It's mass and density evoking a sense of immense gravity like the feeling of a stone falling through an expanse of deep water, falling for infinity. See if you can feel the stone cube below you. See the perfection of its structure, the congruence of all sides and the evenness of all 6 sides. Feel this cube as your throne and feel your noble presence as you sit here.

As the base is steady and solid now you bring your awareness to the space above your head. Imagine a luminous sphere of white light radiating in all directions. Sense it's inherent qualities of connection, expansion, and brilliance.

Now breathe in the base. Slow deep breath. Breathe in the entire world like a vacuum. Bring awareness up the central channel to the crown and exhale slowly radiating out the crown. Repeat this breath three more times. After the last exhale sit and be aware of these to centers at the same time. Practice this often.

These two points, located on the opposite ends of the central channel, act as doorways between your conscious and subconscious worlds, leading to deep insight and freeing blocked energy. These points are neutral, waiting for your command and will unlock their innate power and wisdom as you invoke their symbols. As the Base becomes more complete, it offers more energy and support to the system and as it does this, the sphere at the Crown becomes increasingly radiant, il-

luminating connections from a place of sovereignty, wisdom, and trust.

As the central channel becomes clear, the ability to see that both the good and bad experiences and emotions can be felt in their entirety. We can embody being present and have our full life force available to us.

The "I Am" Statement

Now that you have these symbols in place with the two shapes and two colors, we are going to create an "I Am" statement. This is a simple statement that evokes the experience of your Base and Crown quickly at any time. People utilize a variety of "I Am" statements. You are welcome to choose one from the list provided below or create one of your own.

> I Am Complete.
>
> I Am Flowing.
>
> I Am Sovereign and Connected.
>
> I Am One.
>
> I Am the Light.
>
> I Am Divinity.

We are going to give you the opportunity to go through an exercise to choose what "I Am" statement works best for you. The "I Am" statement can change over time. By choosing a statement that evokes the feelings that arise when your Base active and your Crown is open, the "I Am" statement acts like a button you can push to quickly trigger the connection to this

connected state. When the word or words are chosen precisely, they allow the symbols from the conscious world to open to the subconscious realms and invoke the deep truth of who we are.

Relax your body and bring yourself into this state with Prime breathing. The Base below you is complete, balanced and still, steady and connected to you and only you. Breathe in and feel the Base. Breathe out and feel your Crown radiating. As you expand your awareness into this state, use a "I Am" statement that describes this state. As the word comes to you, complete the "I Am" statement by filling in the blank. For example, you might say, "I Am Complete," or "I Am Sovereign & Connected," or "I Am Divinity," or "I Am The Light," or "I Am Free." Feel this decree permeating your entire being with the truth of your soul and state the decree in its entirety. "I Am _____."

When you get your statement, stop reading and repeat it a few times to yourself. As you practice the I Am statement it should quickly invoke the cube at the base and give you a physical, mental and emotional connection to being on your throne. Sovereign in your world. If it doesn't, repeat this chapter and get one that makes you hum.

As we continue, we will exercise the power of the "I Am" statement and explore more ways to empower the Prime Healing process.

The Mudra

Now that you have practiced the visualization and have found your "I Am" statement, we are going to add a kinetic anchor called a mudra. In Sanskrit, the word mudra means seal, mark, or gesture. While some utilize the entire body, most appear as a unique gesture performed with the hands. These energetic seals can be utilized to affect the flow of energy and consciousness in the body. By incorporating your mudra into your practice, you are gifted a wonderful tool to ground your energetic realignment into the 3D realms with the movement of the body. It is best to combine it with the ones we've just practiced to invoke a state of connection at the Crown and completeness at the Base.

Place the book open on a table in front of you where you can still read it. We will try a few examples but you will eventually find a mudra that works for you. Put your hands in a prayer position in front of you. From that position, allow your hands to twist, bringing one forward and one backwards over each other while maintaining a connection at the base of the hands. As the fingers of the left hand point toward you, the fingers of the right hand rotate in the opposite direction and point away from you. As you rotate your hands, begin to recite your "I Am" statement, concluding the statement as you bring your hands back into their original position of prayer together in front of you. To get the feeling of another mudras, let's try something simple. Clasp your hands together in front of you, in

anyway you choose, and as you begin your statement, pull them apart. Conversely, try starting your statement with your hands apart, bringing them together as you make your decree. Tune into how these forms of movement feel in your body when paired with your "I Am" statement. Now this time, recite your "I Am" statement and allow your body, hands and fingers to intuit a mudra for you. If it doesn't come immediately, take some time with it and feel into how you can use your hands to amplify the feeling of the statement. While the "I Am" statement needs to be empowered with a precise and effective choice of words, you can be more relaxed when choosing your mudra, as it is primarily used to bring the power of the statement into the body and anchor it into physical reality.

The more simple it is, the less noticeable it is, the more comfortable it will be to perform in all situations. A simple version would be touching your pointer and thumb together on each hand. Once you've discovered your mudra, take some time to practice the recitation and movement until it feels completely fluid, memorable and embodied. This can be practiced easily throughout the day. In busy public places like restaurants or at work, you can go through the process just once, reciting the statement quietly or even internally as you perform the mudra. If you'd like to spend some time in meditation, you can lengthen the process, performing the mudra while making your "I Am" statement and then continue to be with it, allowing the power of the movement and words to culminate in your awareness.

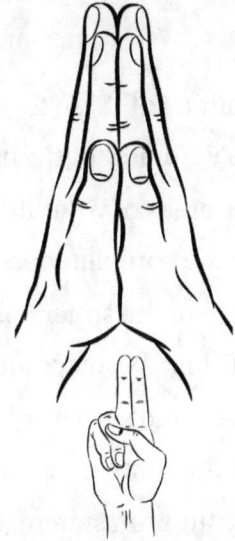

These are examples of classic Madras. The top is the prayer or Anjali Mudra: Many yogis associate Anjali mudra with gratitude, universal connectivity, and equality.

The second, smaller one is the Duality Mudra. This is the Mudra I am using on the cover if this book with my left hand. From my background in Vedic palmistry I've learned that it represents the combining of the opposites of Jupiter and Saturn. The pointer finger is represents Jupiter's qualities of up-lifting into spiritual endeavors. While the middle finger repre-sents Saturn's qualities of bring to Earth and material existence. Combing these opposites into one we have the Duality Mudra.

Saturn   Jupiter

New Patterns.

Now let's put all of these together so that you can re-place old patterns with new patterns. We are going to apply this practice to various areas of your life. As you visualize your Base and Crown, sense the completeness of the cube below you and notice the brilliance of the sphere of white light above you and begin Prime Breathing. As you continue to breathe into your crown and base, begin to say your "I Am" statement internally or out loud and at the same time synchronize the movement of your mudra with your I Am statement.

Practice this short exercise in a variety of situations:

1. Walking in Nature
2. At Work
3. In a Restaurant
4. With Friends
5. With Family
6. Upon Waking Up
7. Right Now

As you find yourself in these situations, practice the ex-ercise, combining the visualization with the "I Am" statement and mudra. The statement does not need to be said aloud and by choosing a simple mudra, the exercise can be done without catching any attention. There's no need to be walking around making grandiose gestures exclaiming, "I am One!". You can

keep it simple and it will be even more effective. The more this is practiced, the easier it is to maintain your consciously connected state with the universe within and all around you.

Seeing the Worst in Yourself

With Prime Healing you will experience the duality in life and in yourself. Hot-cold, good-bad reside in one another and with this exercise you will see that the "worst in you" is also the "best in you". After you get deep and dirty with the left column, go through the Prime Breathing with Hands and see what the opposite looks like in the Crown.

First-Write the "worst" about yourself. Don't hold back, get mean. "Worst"	Prime Breathing	After taking in the "Worst" in the Base see in the Crown the opposite. "Best"
Appearance	Prime Breathe Hands	Appearance
Personality	Prime Breathe Hands	Personality
Life's Purpose	Prime Breathe Hands	Life's Purpose
Relationships	Prime Breathe Hands	Relationships
Personal Power	Prime Breathe Hands	Personal Power

Yup, both columns are true. Reread that right column a few times and let it sink in.

Steps to Practice Prime Healing

You can practice Prime Healing on your own but to fully "do" Prime Healing you need to Practice with someone else. Deep connections are present when you work with another person. This can be in a casual or more office like setting. Paid or not. The point is to walk someone else's psyche through the process of seeing the duality in one of their issues and releasing the blocks.

You would have first had to have had a session and dug deep into your blocks, so this should be easy to assist another person. I have certified myself for practicing the Cube Sovereignty and other elements of Prime Healing and Prime Codex and worked with clients for over 12 months continuously. I have also given permission for 4 others to share the Prime Healing pattern transmission. So while this is challenging it moves it from a mental idea to a reality.

Step 1. Get an in person or Video Session from a Prime Healer Practitioner. That info is at: PrimeHealing.org

Steps for Prime Healing process:

1. Read and digest Prime Healing Book

2. Watch and Complete Online Course

3. Receive a counseling session

4. Give a counseling session

Prime Healing Into Your Future

Now that you have the anchor points we've introduced, I suggest you set aside a dedicated moment in your day to engage in this practice for a longer period of time. By diving into the visualization until it feels palpable and then combining it with your "I Am" statement, you can kinetically ground the cellular memory of this profound state of being by exercising the mudra with full presence of your power. When you continue this longer practice daily, it becomes much easier to evoke and maintain this energized state of empowered sovereignty. You will be able to maintain longer states of feeling the cube at the base and sitting in the presence of being a King or Queen. A practice that is repeated often becomes a habit and a habit that is repeated becomes seamlessly integrated into our daily experience of life as a way of being. If you practice best in the morning, you can simply do this meditation while still resting in bed, or if you prefer, after a cup of tea while perched on your meditation pillow, or on your deck in the rays of the rising sun. It can be done before sleeping, in a bath, or even right in the seat in which you sit at work. Whatever moment of the day is best for you, choose something that feels repeatable and that you can commit to easily. It should be easy to say a few words put your hands in a certain position and feel your base and crown humming. If you can find just one or two minutes in your day, that's all you need to commit to this practice, though five are incredible and if you want to practice ten, that's amazing as

well. Simply visualize the dark cube at your Base and the radiance of your connected Crown. Then declare your "I Am" statement as you animate your moving mudra. Keeping your hands in the finished position for the rest of the meditation. Then bask in the experience, sitting in the presence of your own energy. You can experiment with this practice and make it unique. Feel free to play and experiment. These longer practices times prepares our ability to drawn in blocks in our system and experience the whole truth in our crown.

If you feel stuck or find resistance to your practice, you may have found some attachments that has become ready for your attention. By bringing your open conscious awareness to the resistance with a sense of gratitude, curiosity and acceptance, notice what is tugging and feel into the experience. Perhaps you feel your dad, or some debt you've not yet been able to clear. By activating your practice with your fully embodied intention, these cords can be cleared as well, freeing up more energy for you to gather into yourself and utilize in more effective and enjoyable ways. You can return to the chapter on contracts and go through the exercise, or you can do it on your own in the way you've created. Whether it's a cord with friends and you find resistance to detachment because of fear of losing the friendship, or attachment with a parent, discovering your resistance comes from a time when you needed their help to feel safe, spend some time feeling it and going through the exercises at your own pace. During your longer practice of sitting

on your throne, invite yourself to experience the new connections you've created by relieving your Base from the attachment and consciously intending the energy to rise up into the
sphere of light at your crown. Enjoy the majesty of your Crown's
brilliance and wisdom providing a way for you to authentically
and enjoyably connect to the universe that surrounds you.

CHAPTER THIRTEEN

The Paradox

"If you can let your experience happen, it will release its knots and unfold, leading to a deeper, more grounded experience of yourself."   *-John Welwood*

Prime healing is a potent tool that can be used to release many long-standing blocks. But there are deep blocks in most of us that are very hard to unearth. These blocks are called the paradox. They carry so much intensity that we find ways to block and avoid these areas of our lives. It is paradoxical because these areas of our lives are also some of the most important things for us.

Let's use the example of a student of Prime Healing. Lynn is a 34-year-old woman living in Northern California. When she first came to work with Prime Healing, she was very shy socially and was working a job that paid the bills but gave her no pride or satisfaction. She dedicated herself to working deeply with Prime Breathing and the Four Ceremonies and was able to get her 8-year-old and 14-year-old back to sovereignty and release many blocks with her social phobias.

Her life shifted quickly and as she was able to find her sovereign Base. She felt herself having precious new moments of enjoying being around people and was amazed that she even was flirty and open with new people. By the third session, we had started working with the 18-year-old. As we opened the ceremony, it was obvious that her 18-year-old's Base was corded and had many active blocks and the Crown was barely open. As we worked with the 18-year-old, the story came out that she had really wanted to help people and possibly even get training in healing arts but because her 8-year-old was still corded to her Mom, she let her mother's belief that healing work is "the devil's work" affect her inner cosmology. She was holding onto a belief rooted in her Catholic background that she would be shunned by her family if she did this type of work. She felt the sting of being shunned when she was in early primary school. Being from an Indian family she was made fun of by a group of girls at school and began to avoid any experience that she felt would lead to her feeling excluded.

We talked about what she thought of healers. She had little experience and talked openly about how she thought they were kooks and witches. By being a good little girl to her mother, she adopted beliefs and a lifestyle that was not hers. There was the paradox. She had judged healers when in fact it was an important part of her life. As we proceeded to breathe through the blocks and circulate her whole truth, the healer in her started to unveil. With tears in her eyes, she began to share that she could really feel her heart's authentic desire to help people.

Through Prime Healing, she became open to a new point of view. She realized that healing is simply accepting all parts of ourselves and allowing our whole truth to be present.

Lynn is now learning how to guide people with Prime Healing and has a sweet and sensitive nature that is unfolding her heart's true path. She continues to work to accept all parts of herself and create her own unique path. She was even able to share with her mom and dad about her practice to help people find freedom and to her surprise, they shared that they thought it sounded like a good thing for her.

You can see from Lynn that when we block our pains to protect ourselves, we also block our gifts. The bigger the gift, the deeper and scarier the blocks. This makes life an adventurous treasure hunt. The prize is our deepest gifts to share with the world. Our adversaries are actually our worst fears and nightmares. Prime Healing offers a road map on this journey to wholeness and victory.

You can see from the following diagram that the process is simple. Unblock all connections from the Base and let all your energy return back to Base. Then allow it to flow up the center of the body and connect outwards from the sun at the Crown. The process is simple and prepares us to go deeper and deeper into our fears and hurt places, but the deeper we go the more potent the work is.

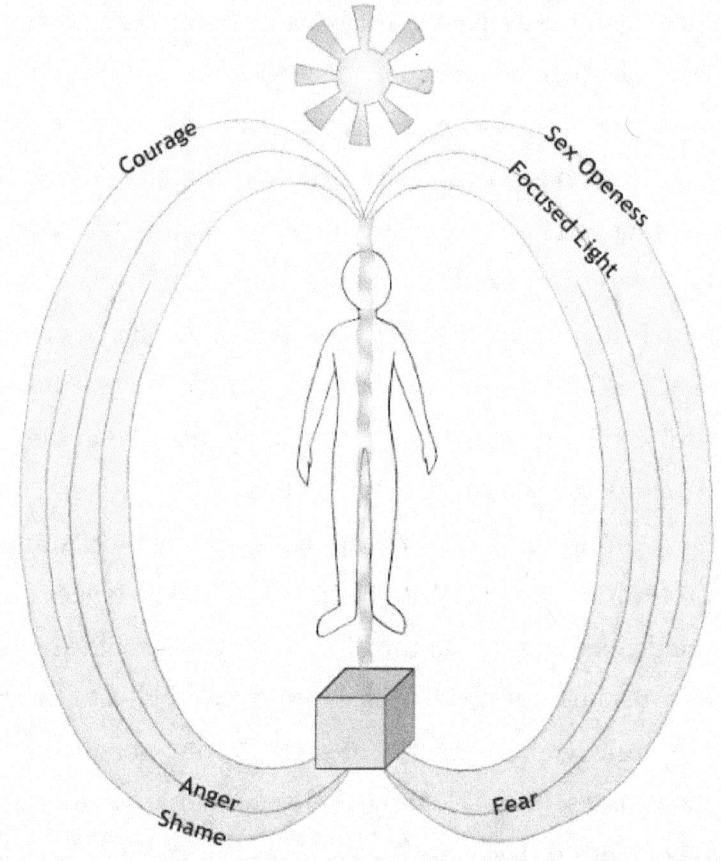

When any block is accepted fully and allowed to flow through the central channel to the Crown, we experience the Whole Truth.

Abundance-includes-Greed
Courage-includes-Fear
Pride-includes-Shame
Connection-includes-Loneliness

The world is in duality and once we can accept all parts of ourselves, we no longer block experiences like pain, fear, guilt and shame. We are able to be with these moments fully and allow the whole truth to be present in us as us.

When we experience the whole truth and our base is sovereign, our brain can finally relax, thereby ending mental brain loops with the awareness that trusting in our sovereign base keeps us safe connected and on our path.

The gift of clarity and peace we receive by ending the emotional loops of trauma is now ours. We accept and appreciate traumas from the past and see the whole story. When we are brave enough to feel and pull every last bit of trauma back into the dense black base, the emotional loops can finally end leaving us steady and open to life.

The Whole Truth sets us free.

CHAPTER FOURTEEN

The Road Ahead

"Throughout the first stage of surrender, we respect the gravity of our feelings, acknowledge each thought, belief, or conclusion as having a right to exist, and welcome each experience—no matter how surreal, one-sided, or distasteful it seems."

— Matt Kahn

Allow this process to unfold naturally, with a sense of enjoyment and trust. As you practice, allow the ritual to feel playful and fun. It's likely that by now, you've had the experience of feeling your Base free from cords and have enjoyed the wonderful sense of completeness and sovereignty that results. Hopefully, you can sense the true connection that comes through attuning to life through the Crown. With the stronger awareness that arises through practice, you will become more adept at sitting on your cube like a noble King/ Queen of light.

You may begin noticing wobbles at the Base when you share space and time with other people. Perhaps when you are around your mother, you'll feel some tugging at your Base from years of ingrained patterning still being practiced by her. Maybe your lover feels a need for connection and reaches out by tugging at your Base. As your awareness begins to expand, you'll likely find yourself reading the energy of others. As a helpful human, you may find yourself called to offer some guidance as to how to restructure the energetic system of connection. You may find it's easier to share what results you've experienced and then just share the process by sharing this book. Enjoy the process and allow this to also unfold naturally.

It can be fun to experiment with the visualizations. For example, you can play with opening up your Base, attaching into something, allowing the feelings that arise to be felt and then releasing the cords, dissolving contracts and reclaiming the energy back into your Base to fuel better connections through the Crown.

As you play and expand yourself into more experiences of Prime Healing, you'll find yourself increasingly agile at negotiating tugs at the base, no longer reacting as you may have in the past. With the keen awareness of your own energetic system, you'll skillfully navigate previously triggering relationships with more ease and grace. By creating your own visualizations, you'll strengthen your ability to maintain this state, attuning to the subtle awareness of yourself. You may even catch yourself off balance and you'll have the confidence to quickly rework the wobbles into a self-created harmonious state.

Questions & Answers

Q: How can I learn more about Prime Healing?
A: Easy, go to PrimeHealing.org.

Q: Is the point of Prime Healing to experience all life interactions, relationships and situations through the crown?
A: In short, yes. But it runs a little deeper than that too. I'm explaining everything in the simplest way possible and when we look at the Crown and the Base, we recognize that they are mir-

rors of each other. So actually, by connecting at the Crown, we give the Base an opportunity to function at its best. So indeed, yes, we are aiming to experience life through our connections at the crown, but we don't need to constantly work on money, or perfect each and every relationship, or micromanage every situation that arises. All we have to do is just bring it up into the Crown. Nothing has to be perfected at all. We all tried that, that's the old way and it never worked, did it? It's like herding cats. You get one going towards the door and the other one jumps on the counter. Another one jumps on your head. The little one sneaks out the door. You finally get them all in one place and one of them makes a run for it. It never stops. That's life, it's always moving, always surprising, always offering a wild card. That's the point! We are here to experience it all. In fact, all we are doing in this work is changing our experience to perceive and interact with things exactly as they are by tuning into them with the higher degree of conscious awareness, we are playing the game instead of the game playing us. We can allow the attachments to dissolve, we bring one thing at a time up into the crown, allowing a natural pace to guide the process. When the subsequent fear, anger, grasping, shame and anxiety that once arose as a result of the attachment is dissolved and the mechanism that created it is dismantled, our ability to function and perceive the world more clearly invites us to finally experience the reality of life in a whole new way. Our truth becomes clearer. Our awareness grows keen and our relationships become a lot more fun. Life feels more exciting and we

find ourselves putting more trust in it. Even when things don't turn out the way we expect, we sense that life has our back and we find ourselves curious about what's around the corner instead of bitter about what was left behind. We trust ourselves and we trust in the experience we have with others, even the challenging ones.

Q: What if an issue stays stuck in the base?

A: This is common for many people. There are issues that are withheld from clearing mostly because they think by holding on to them, they will kept safe. It's that primal phase between 0-7 that creates the paradigm that sets the stage for the resistance. Do you recall a time when you were terrified of a monster in the closet or a ghost outside the window, or something scary under the bed? Do you remember hiding under the blankets, pulling the sheets up over your eyes, hoping that would save you? Or did you make a run for your mom's room, convinced she would save you? Now we know that there actually was never a monster in the closet. With our matured awareness and more keen awareness of our energy field, we can see that it was our root being open that set us up to feel unsafe and unsure about the world. To stay safe, people feel like they need to keep this contract they've held onto and that by maintaining it, it might even keep them from dying. These are old contracts we developed when we were very young. When you encounter one of these, gently release it and see if you're safe without it. Ask yourself if you're safe with it corded at the Base and when it's

brought to the Crown, see how that feels in regards to safety. Notice the difference in your emotions and your body. The actual experience of feeling real safety will inform your subconscious that this contract is no longer necessary and the need for it to be in place will dissolve naturally. Other times, people maintain these contracts because they are unaware that they exist. For example, if someone had an abusive father, they may have made the contract that they needed to fight him off and keep their guard up at all times to keep themselves safe from the random bouts of anger and spontaneous violence. In order to be aware of them, cords were sent from the Base to the father, so they could feel what was going to happen before it happened, so they could run before the abuse could occur. The primal self protects the contract, keeping it stuck in place, because it senses the need for it for survival. However, through the practice of Prime Healing and connecting through the Crown, we actually become even more perceptive and aware, sensing much more acutely and accurately into the reality of the world around us. It could even be true that this contract was made with a person who is no longer alive, yet the contract continues to run its outdated programming. In the case that the person, say the father we spoke of, is actually still living, with a clear root and connected crown, a conversation could be invited that could prove illuminating and healing.

Q: Would you recommend someone also include therapy/counseling in addition to doing this work?

A: For sure. Anything that can help us experience and bring to our awareness our blocks is beneficial. Many people find other healing techniques work better when they have a basic under-standing of how to work with the Prime Healing process.

Q: Is it beneficial to cord to my own body?

A: This is another great question. When I began to do the Prime Healing process myself, I thought that it was obviously healthy and helpful to have a cord to my own body. But as furthered my exploration of my energetic system, I began to find flaws in this belief. While working with one of my teachers, I had the real-ization that it was best for me to release the attachment that I had connected to everything, even my own body. I invite you to explore the experience of closing your Base completely.

Envision your body and notice your Base. Find the cord that connects you to your physical body. As you follow it to its origin, release the cord and allow that energy to rise into your Crown. Bring your awareness to the Base residing beneath you. Focus your attention on the integrity of its structure and the feel the density and strength of the black stone. See how it is perfectly balanced, unblemished, free of holes and cords as you look closely at the top, bottom and all of its remaining four sides. Visualize your Base and see that it is perfectly stable and unwaveringly still and then bring your attention again to your Crown. Allow yourself to see your Crown as it forges a beautiful connection with your body and notice how that feels.

I had an amazing experience the first time I connected to my body through the Crown. I felt at ease and in tune with myself. I found the idea of aging suddenly much different than I had before. I felt harmony and peace with my age. I was 42 years of age at the time and I realized that everyone who was lucky enough to live as long as I had would be 42 at some point and I could feel a sincere joy at the idea of being 42. It felt great to connect to my body through the Crown and much more harmonious this way.

Q: Is Prime Healing a form of Spiritual Bypassing?

A: The word bypass sounds like a way of skipping a step. This process lays the foundation for us to have an opportunity to experience a life that feels innately spiritual. In my mind, the word "spiritual" evokes a sense of divinity and the infinite essence of who we truly are beyond any restrictions related to time, form, situation, name or structure. Prime Healing isn't designed to negate the spirit or superficially skip over something as the word bypass suggests. It is the initial step. By firming up the Base, leaks and cords that once drained us no longer do. Instead, the reclamation of energy provides an ample boost of renewed vigor and joy and we can engage with the universe in a more authentic way, more aware of ourselves as spiritual beings inhabiting human bodies. When we are corded at the Base, we react quickly and we find ourselves extremely vigilant about our need to protect and promote ourselves. It's easy to forget who we truly are when we are fighting to simply exist.

When we relax into a state of conscious connectivity, we are perpetually reminded of our magic and the magic of the world around us. With the support of a sovereign base, this "spiritual" experience becomes sustained, steady, normal and real.

Q: Can I do too much Prime Healing?
A: Prime Healing is a healthy, normal, sustainable process and unless you choose to focus on it so much that you ignore other important areas of your life, it's something that is safe to practice consistently. If you have lots of free time to practice, that's great. You are welcome to dive into extended meditations on the work if that suits you. Because Prime Healing feels so inspiring and helpful, new students often want to share their experience and talk about the process with everyone around them. At the beginning of your exploration into Prime Healing, it's best to focus on your own process. It would be best to wait to assist others with theirs, as focused training provides a much deeper relationship with the work and a more enhanced ability to navigate how to share it effectively with others as a guide and teacher.

Q: What about the heart?
A: I'm glad you asked. I know a lot of spiritual practices do put the majority of the focus on the heart. When we practice Prime Healing, our focus is primarily centered on the function, structure and relationship between the energetic centers residing above and below the physical body. When the Base is clear and

the Crown is open for connection, the heart acts as a moderator of the beautiful dynamic that is potentiated by the flow of energy shared between these two points. We will explore so much more about the power of the heart in Books 2 & 3. For now though, it's important that we lay a good foundation with a well-functioning structure on which to build. As you master the integrity of the energetic dynamics arising from your Base to illuminate your Crown, you'll begin to naturally discover how potent and important it is to fully actualize this first step in the process. This method primes the energetic system for all the work that follows. It's important that we trust in the natural evolution, allowing the newly chosen state of being to become fully integrated.

In Closing

My intention is that this book provides you some insight and effective tools which you can utilize to navigate your own energetic system with conscious awareness. With your newfound awareness and sensitivity to reworking blocks and connections, you've gained the ability to bring the tug-of-war to a close. Instead of life pulling us it guides us and we are open to experiencing whatever life brings.

Beyond this book, I want to offer you more. Provided below are links to videos and workshops. I hope you'll join me both online and in person so I can share the love and enthusiasm I have for this work. During the live events, we will have

the opportunity to practice and learn ways to offer this work for the benefit of others.

At this point though, you've already been provided everything you need to make this work your own. As you evolve it into something of your own, it will become even more powerful and effective. You've been given full artistic license to customize the process as you wish and to rework the wording and imagery to something that suits you. You can make the cube the size of the earth or as little as you like. As you offer your own imagination, style, color and flavor, Prime Healing becomes something that works even better for you, because it was created and tested for and by you. You can make the statements more elaborate, the mudras more powerful, the visualizations more elaborate and clear. You're the King/Queen of your world and it's all up to you. Do what you want and be who you are. Enjoy the duality of life and looking into the great mystery with an unbound mind and open heart.

PRIME HEALING

ABOUT THE AUTHOR

To Learn more go to:

PrimeHealing.org

www.ingramcontent.com/pod-product-compliance
Lightning Source LLC
Chambersburg PA
CBHW062209280526
45788CB00001B/506

* 9 7 8 1 0 9 9 9 3 2 1 4 4 *